W9-BNP-365

Ready-to-Use Activities for Before and After School Programs

Verna Stassevitch
Patricia Stemmler
Rita Shotwell
Marian Wirth

Illustrations by Patricia Stemmler

JOSSEY-BASS
A Wiley Imprint
www.josseybass.com

Published by Jossey-Bass
A Wiley Imprint
989 Market Street, San Francisco, CA 94103-1741   www.josseybass.com

Jossey-Bass books and products are available through most bookstores. To contact Jossey-Bass directly call our Customer Care Department within the U.S. at 800-956-7739, outside the U.S. at 317-572-3986 or fax 317-572-4002.

Jossey-Bass also publishes its books in a variety of electronic formats. Some content that appears in print may not be available in electronic books.

Library of Congress Cataloging-in-Publication Data
Ready-to-use activities for before and after school programs/Verna
Stassevitch...[et al.];[illustrations by Patricia Stemmler].

     p. cm.
    Includes index.
    ISBN 0-87628-691-0 (spiral)   ISBN 0-87628-120-X (paper)
      1. Creative activities and seat work.   2. Handicrafts.   3. Games.
4. Day care centers—Activity programs.   I. Stassevitch, Verna
GV1203.R37   1989   89-30567
372.13'078—dc19

FIRST EDITION
PB Printing 10 9 8 7

About the Authors

The four authors have written an earlier book entitled *Musical Games, Fingerplays and Rhythmic Activities for Early Childhood* (Parker Publishing Company, West Nyack, N.Y., 1983.)

Verna Stassevitch received Bachelor of Science and Bachelor of Music degrees from Skidmore College. She has pursued further study at the graduate level in Orff Schulwerk training. She was supervisor of music in Newburyport, Massachusetts, for two years and director of music at The Wilson School in St. Louis, Missouri, for twelve years. Ms. Stassevitch has been headmistress of The Wilson School since 1975. She has presented many workshops for teachers, and has taught beginning and intermediate Orff music classes at Fontbonne College in St. Louis and early childhood music classes at St. Louis Community College at Forest Park. She has also served as consultant and instructor in a special program (correlating music and language) at the Miriam School in St. Louis, serving children with learning disabilities. She is president of the Missouri Independent Schools Association, member of the Board of Directors of the Missouri Council for American Private Education and past president of the Educational Confederation of Metropolitan St. Louis.

Pat Stemmler (the book's illustrator as well as a co-author) studied music education at Butler University, and has been teaching music and art to preschool and primary age children for the last 15 years. Currently she is teaching at the Ladue Early Childhood Center in St. Louis. She has given many music workshops in the St. Louis area. Illustrating has been her hobby for many years, and she has designed logos for the Coalition for the Environment, the St. Louis Association for the Education of Young Children, and the St. Louis Chapter of the American Orff-Schulwerk Association.

Rita Shotwell received her Bachelor of Arts in Communications from St. Louis University, a Master of Arts in Teaching Early Childhood from Webster University, St. Louis, and Basic Certification in Rhythmic Movement and Folk Dance Curriculum from Phyllis Weikart and the High/Scope Foundation. She has training in the Orff and Kodaly approaches to teaching music to children. She is a part-time instructor for St. Louis Community College at Meramec and is an early childhood music teacher at Community School and several other St. Louis area schools, working with children one year old to first grade. She conducts toddler/parent music classes at the Center of Contemporary Arts and teaches senior citizens in the Arts for Heart Program. She has worked with the children at Shriner's Hospital for Crippled Children and the St. Louis Society for Crippled Children. She has given many workshops for educators at local, state, regional and national meetings. She is the author of *Rhythm and Movement Activities* and *New Words, Old*

Tunes published by Alfred Publishing Company in California, and has written an article on intergenerational programs for the *Orff Echo*, a national quarterly magazine. She is a member of the local and national American Orff-Schulwerk Association, local and national Association for the Education of Young Children, Child Day Care Association, Midwest Kodaly Association, and National Association for Childhood Education International. She is past president of the St. Louis Orff chapter, and also the St. Louis Suburban Association of Childhood Education.

Marian Wirth received a Bachelor of Science in Education from Ohio State University and a Master of Arts in Learning Disabilities from St. Louis University. She taught perceptual motor skills at the Miriam School in St. Louis for eight years and was an early childhood education specialist with the Child Day Care Association for four and one half years. She has taught child development classes at St. Louis Community College and has given numerous workshops for teachers. Mrs. Wirth is the author of *Teacher's Handbook of Children's Games: A Guide to Developing Perceptual Motor Skills*. This book has been published in paperback under the title, *Games for Growing Children*, Parker Publishing Company, W. Nyack, New York.

About This Resource

Ready-to-Use Activities for Before and After School Programs gives teachers and supervisors in extended-day programs a unique store of high-quality yet easy-to-do activities that are both challenging and relaxing for children. The 200 activities included are clearly presented so that many students can complete them independently. Moreover, they will help you give children a *choice* of activities, which is particularly important *after* school.

For easy selection and use, all of these ready-to-use activities are organized into six sections and printed in a big $8\frac{1}{2} \times 11$ inch format that folds flat for photocopying of the directions pages. The six sections include:

1. **ARTS AND CRAFTS**—thirty-seven stimulating projects covering a wide range of creative media, including painting, cutting, collage, construction, sandcasting, sculpture, printing, weaving, puppet-making, and more.

2. **INDOOR AND OUTDOOR GAMES**—forty-four active or quiet games, including language games, ball bouncing, rope jumping, relays, and favorite group games such as "Man from Mars," "Indian Ball," and "Mouse Trap."

3. **SONGS AND FINGERGAMES**—thirty-eight child-tested favorites or originals, such as "Wiggle-Waggle," "Hand Jive Routines," "Riddle Song," "Barnyard Song," and "I Am Special."

4. **SCIENCE AND NATURE**—twenty-one unforgettable projects that are easy to do; for example, constructing an incubator for hatching eggs, creating musical instruments, and building three different types of bird feeders.

5. **HEALTHY SNACKS**—thirty-five snacks children can prepare cooperatively while expanding their arithmetic skills and nutrition facts; for example, "Banana Boats," "Peanut Butter Reindeer," "Sandwich Cut-Outs," and "Fruit Kabobs."

6. **SPECIAL ACTIVITIES**—twenty-five humorous stories to act out, filmstrip and slide shows, card games with regular cards, and useful knots.

The age range for each activity is indicated in the Table of Contents and on the activity directions page, except when the activity may be applicable for all ages, such as snack preparation and songs. Many projects reach upwards to grades 5 and 6 (ages 11 or 12). Most of the projects and activities may be used in mixed age groups, or by one or two children alone. (The teacher should use her/his judgment as to which children can work independently.)

Here are some special features of this resource that will work for you:

- Activities that are very easy to do are asterisked in the Table of Contents and "stamped" EASY-TO-DO on the directions page.

- Safety instructions, wherever appropriate, are highlighted in bold type.

- Any materials needed are generally inexpensive and readily available.
- The arts and crafts projects produce attractive results without being "cutesy." They encourage children to be creative rather than to follow a single prescribed pattern.
- The games are exciting but essentially noncompetitive. They present a welcome change from the academic school day.
- Many of the snack recipe, card game, and humorous story directions pages can be reproduced for children to take home.
- Some of the projects in Sections I, IV, and VI can be started on one day and continued for several succeeding days, for example, "Paperbag Building Blocks," "Constructing a Cold Frame," and "Filmstrips."
- A number of the activities such as fingergames (Section III) are especially suitable for preschoolers.

We believe these games, projects, and activities can help create a well-rounded and inviting extended-day program whether it be in a school setting, a day care center, or at home. The activities are also suitable for use with Scout groups and in summer camp, family day care, and recreational programs.

Our special thanks to the staff and children of The Wilson School for sharing many creative ideas with us.

Verna Stassevitch
Patricia Stemmler
Rita Shotwell
Marian Wirth

Contents

* = Easy-to-Do Activities.

Cutting and Collage • 37–43

*Fringe Cutting *(3 and 4 years)* • 37
Paper Snowflakes *(4–11 years)* • 38
Paper Doll Chains *(4–11 years)* • 39
*Collage: Three Types *(3–11 years)* • 40
*Magazine Collage *(3–10 years)* • 42
*Torn Paper Pictures *(3–11 years)* • 43

Printing • 44–47

*Sponge Printing *(3–10 years)* • 44
Potato Printing *(3–11 years)* • 45
Monoprinting *(4–11 years)* • 46
Styrofoam Printing *(5–10 years)* • 47

2. INDOOR AND OUTDOOR GAMES 49

Ball-Bouncing Activities • 50–53

*Bouncing Ball *(5–12 years)* • 50
*Wall Ball *(6 years and up)* • 51
*Bounce and Bounce *(8 years and up)* • 52
*One, Two, Three O'Leary *(8 years and up)* • 53

Rope-Jumping Activities • 54–58

Cinderella *(6 years and up)* • 54
Teddy Bear *(6 years and up)* • 54
Down in the Valley *(6 years and up)* • 55
I Was Born in a Frying Pan *(6 years and up)* • 55
First and Second Grade *(6 years and up)* • 55
Bobby Bear *(6–9 years)* • 56
Mabel Able *(6 years and up)* • 57
Rock' N' Roll Kid *(8 years and up)* • 58

Indoor Games • 59–74

*Tiger Ball *(2–4 years)* • 59
*Bean Bag Bowling *(3–11 years)* • 60
Bean Bag Shuffleboard *(6–12 years)* • 61
*Balloon Badminton *(3½ to 10 or 12 years)* • 62
Pom-Pom Paddle Ball *(7–11 years)* • 63
*Freddie the Frog *(4–6 years)* • 64
*Jump Over the Brook *(4–10 years)* • 65

Humorous Short Stories to Act Out • 224–235

Useful Knots (8 years and up) • 236 239

1

ARTS
and
CRAFTS

Generally, extended-day arts and crafts should be available on a free-choice basis. For young children, some help by the teacher (or by older children), may be needed in starting. For older children, an introduction may be all that is necessary.

Open-ended art emphasizes the process, not the product. This way, young children can participate at an elementary level, and older ones can work in a complex way with the same materials. Of course, each child's own style is unique and beautiful.

Through arts and crafts, children develop their fine motor skills, their creativity, and their problem-solving abilities. Each project also teaches something about science, as basic materials are used to create and transform.

Q-Tip™ Painting

(Homemade Markers)

Ages: 3–8 years

Materials & Equipment: Food coloring

Q-tips® or other cotton swabs (at least one per color, preferably two)

Plastic lid or saucer

Typing, drawing, or any kind of paper to draw on

Smocks for children

Directions: Children should wear smocks to prevent staining clothes. Ideally, the group should consist of not more than four children.

Place a few drops of three or four colors (undiluted), in separate places around the plastic lid or saucer. Each color has its own cotton swab near it. Children then dip and draw.

The emphasis should be on children's exploring color effects rather than creating a finished product.

After initial exploration with undiluted colors, the teacher can place a cup of water near the color palette; then children can explore diluting the colors by dipping the cotton swab in water as well as color. They can also mix colors on paper for different effects.

Comments: This project presents an interesting discovery experience for any age.

Face Painting

Ages: 3–11 years

Materials: Water colors; water

At least one small brush (several are better)

For very detailed designs, a cosmetic brush is useful.

Paper towels

Directions: Pre-dampen the water colors by brushing a few drops of water over each square in the tray. Let the colors soak about five minutes. Paint should be thick so it doesn't drip.

The painter should first practice on his or her own hand. Then put four or five designs on a piece of paper and let children pick the one they want. They enjoy having a choice.

Comments: Children love having their faces painted for festive occasions, such as Valentine's Day (a heart), Saint Patrick's Day (a shamrock), or to celebrate a special birthday (a flower, rainbow or teddy bear). A skull and crossbones is a delight for Hallowe'en. Any small, simple design can be used.

Some children are hesitant about having paint put on their faces, but almost all will be happy with a design on the back of the hand. It may help a hesitant child to be last in line; after he or she sees all the other children's face designs, it becomes much easier to accept. Colors wash off easily with a little soap and water.

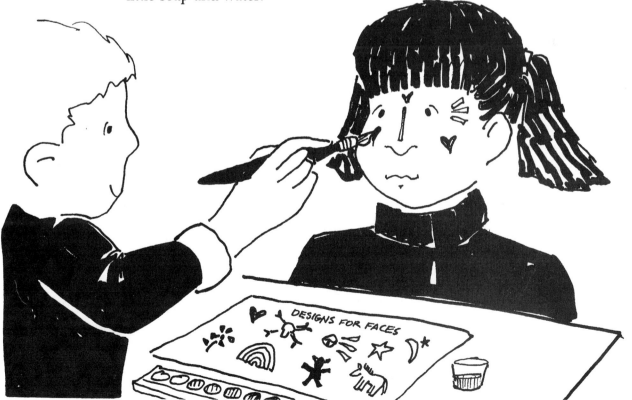

Paper Towel Designs

Ages: 3–11 years

Materials & Equipment: White paper towels (without designs)
Containers about the size of coffee cups, one for each color
Food coloring in several colors
A spoon for each cup
Newspapers
Smocks

Directions: About four children could work at once.

Cover the table with thick newspapers and have children put smocks on to prevent their clothing from being stained.

Put about five drops of food coloring in the bottom of each cup. Fill two-thirds full with warm water. Stir the colors with the spoons.

Place cups in the middle of the table, with space between. Give each child a paper towel, which should be folded into quarters, at least. The more folds, the more complex the design will be. Dip the folded corners into whatever colors children want. The dyes should not be mixed or overlapped while learning the technique. The corners will drip into the cup or onto the newspapers.

Unfold towels and look at the designs. If children want more color, they may refold the towel and dip corners again (in the same or a different way); or, they can use the spoons to place drops of dye on the folded towel in different locations. The dye will soak through all layers to maintain a symmetrical design.

Variation: *Tie-dyed paper towels*

Hold up a left fist, with pointer finger extended straight up. Drape a paper towel over the pointed finger and hand. Grab the towel around the left forefinger with the right hand so that the towel gathers into folds, and lift the towel off the left finger and hand. Tie the gathered towel in two places with yarn. There will be a point at the top and some points at the bottom of the towel. Dip the top points in one color, and the bottom points in another color.

With the spoon, drip some dye in the middle or fold the towel so the middle area can be dipped. This should provide a circular pattern when the towel is unfolded.

Put the finished towels in a large, protected area of the floor with newspapers underneath to dry.

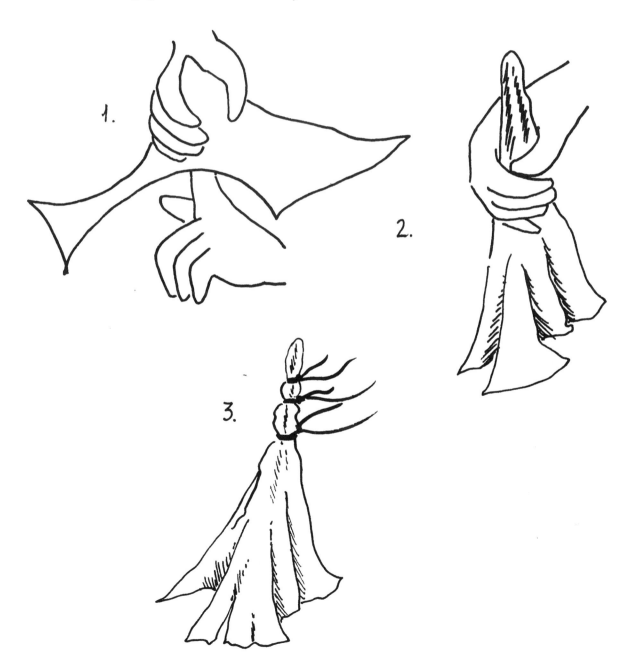

Fingerpaint Slates

Ages: 3–10 years

Materials: Large Zip-loc® bags
Masking tape
Finger paint or fingerpaint substitute (see comments)

Directions: Place three heaping tablespoons of fingerpaint inside Zip-loc® bag.
Flatten bag on table to remove as much air as possible and close top securely.
Tape the top of the bag to make sure that it will remain closed.
Have children use both hands to flatten and spread fingerpaint out smoothly inside the bag. Children may then draw designs into the color by pressing with their finger.
Smear the fingerpaint flat again to erase the design.

Comments: An inexpensive substitute for fingerpaint can be made by combining into an uncooked paste: corn starch, water, and food coloring. Fingerpaint slates help develop the tactile sense and provide some experimentation with liquids.

Fingerprint Pictures

Ages: 5–10 years

Materials & Equipment: Small pieces of drawing paper
Stamp pad
Colored drawing markers

Directions: Cut 8½-by-11-inch drawing paper into six pieces or use 3-by-five-inch cards, if available.

Have child make a clean fingerprint on the paper using a stamp pad and pressing. (This activity all by itself intrigues younger children.)

Once the fingerprint is made, have child study it for a moment to see if they can visualize it as part of an animal.

Use the marking pen to draw all of the details needed to complete the pictures.

Comments: Older children may want to design a few note cards using fingerprint pictures. This project will stimulate children's humorous imaginations.

Crayon Resist

Ages: 5 years and up

Materials: Crayons or, better, oil crayons. The latter are available at art supply stores. Oil crayons are a little more expensive than crayons, but produce a more satisfactory drawing.

Water colors and brush

Drawing paper

Directions: Children should draw a picture using the lighter and brighter crayon colors (e.g., red, green, blue). The lines should be strong and heavy. The picture can consist of a design, scribble-scrabble, or a representational drawing.

When the drawing is complete, make a solution of brown or black watercolor and water. The paint should be of a watery consistency. Paint over the entire drawing. The crayon drawing resists the paint and glows through the dark background.

Comments: The crayon resist technique is particularly suitable for night-time pictures. Children think it's magical that the paint cannot cover the drawing.

All children will make discoveries about mixing wax and water. Older children in particular can achieve some very unusual and artistic effects.

The oil crayons are better for dramatic results.

Beanbags (or Beanbag Construction)

Ages: For any child who can use a stapler (age 4 up) or a needle and thread (age 5 up)

Materials & Equipment: Any heavy material such as denim, cotton duck, or felt

Stapler(s) and/or needle(s) and thread

Filler: dried beans, peas, or small gravel (chat)

Directions: Each child should have a small piece of material, folded in half, wrong side out. It can be pre-cut for very young children into any shape. Five-year-olds (and up) can cut their own if the scissors are sharp. Cut the shape quite a bit larger than you want the beanbag, to allow for one-half-inch seams all around and to allow for filling.

Staple or sew around two-thirds of the edge. One-third should be left open so that the fabric can be turned inside out. Stitches should be fairly small and tight to provide a strong seam. Staples, if used, should overlap, but don't be too fussy about how the beanbag looks.

After turning the material inside out, fill *loosely* with beans, peas or gravel. (There should be room for the fingertips to grip the bag.) **Caution: Supervise the handling of beans, etc., so that children do not get them into nose or mouth.**

Next, it is necessary to sew or staple the last one-third of the seam closed. Children can use an overcast stitch, if they are able, or staple the seam closed, overlapping the staples to prevent any beans, etc. from slipping out.

Variations: Instead of beans or peas, the bags can be stuffed with tissue paper or kleenex. These light-weight "beanbags" are safe to throw in small spaces.

Comments: Few toys are as versatile as the lowly beanbag. They can be used to play hopscotch or tossed at basket, paper, or hula-hoop targets. They can be used to play Beanbag Bowling (page 60), Beanbag Shuffleboard (page 61), and Freddie the Frog (page 64). Another activity children love: Place a long (about 10-inch) wooden block on top of a small block. Place a beanbag on one end of the long block. Children can stamp on the other end of the long block, sending the beanbag flying. Then, try to catch the beanbag.

Backstrap Loom Weaving

Ages: 7–10 years

**Materials
& Equipment:** Large plastic lid (such as from a gallon ice cream container)
Ice pick
Yarn (2 colors)
3-by-5-inch card
string

Directions: *To make loom:* The teacher does this job.

Heat ice pick over candle or gas flame and, using the hot metal, make the following pattern of holes and slots in the plastic lid:

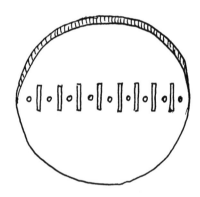

(Please note: Slots should be about 1½-inch in length and lined evenly across the center of the lid. It may help to draw guidelines with a marker. It is important that you begin with a hole and end with a hole, as illustrated.)

To weave: Children can do their own preparations.

Using two colors of yarn (one color for holes, one color for slots), cut enough 36-inch lengths of yarn to place one length in each hole and slot. (This is called "warping" the loom. The yarn running through the holes and slots make up the "warp.")

Once all slots and holes are filled, tie a knot at both ends of the warp, as illustrated.

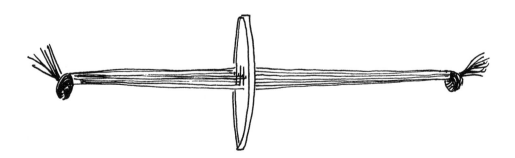

The 3-by-5-inch card will be used as a shuttle. Children may choose either of the two colors (or a third color if available) of yarn to put on the shuttle. This yarn will be the "weft." Cut a piece of yarn about five yards long and wrap it lengthwise around the card shuttle as illustrated:

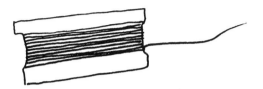

Take two pieces of string and tie one piece around each knot at the end of the warp. Then using the string, tie one end of the warp to a doorknob or heavy table, and tie the other end of the warp to the child! (The string goes around the child's waist or to a belt or over his or her shoulder; this is why it is called *backstrap* loom.) See illustration.

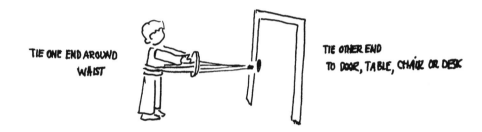

The child must lean back enough to keep the warp taut. Tie the loose end of the weft yarn on the shuttle to the outside yarn of the warp. You're finally ready to begin weaving.

Holding the shuttle in one hand, push down on the plastic lid with the other hand. You will notice a triangular gap in front of the plastic lid. See illustration.

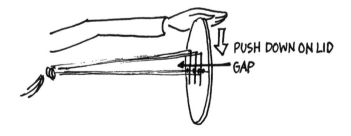

Slide the shuttle through the gap and release pressure on the lid. Pull the plastic lid toward you to "pack" the weft tightly. Now pull *up* on the lid—and slide the shuttle through the gap. Continue weaving alternating *pushing down,* and *pulling up* as you slide the shuttle through the gap. Remember to pull the lid forward after each pass to pack the weft and create a tight weave.

When enough has been woven so that the child's arms barely reach the plastic lid, untie the warp from the child and roll the woven section to make the warp shorter, then retie warp to child and continue to weave.

Card Weaving

Ages: 5–10 years

Materials: Cardboard (see size in directions)
White string or twine
Colored yarn
Scissors

Directions: Cardboard can be cut from boxes or scraps of heavy poster board. (Frame shops will often donate their scrap to schools.) An 8-by-8-inch board would be a good size, but size is not important. Almost anything will work.

Cut ½-inch slots at the top and bottom of the cardboard square, making an effort to line them up vertically. For younger children a wide distance (¾-inch) between slots makes weaving easier—older children will do well with slots closer together (¼-inch apart). There should be an uneven number of slots, but of course, the same on top as on the bottom. **Supervise the use of scissors.**

Taking the string, tie a large knot in the end, and slide the knot into the slot in the upper left corner of the cardboard. Pull the string tight and straight down to the corresponding slot on the bottom left corner; slide the string into the slot—the first warp string is now in place. Bring the string up the rear side to the second slot on the top—as you pull it through the slot pull it tight and straight down to the second bottom slot. Continue in this manner until all slots are strung.

WARP:

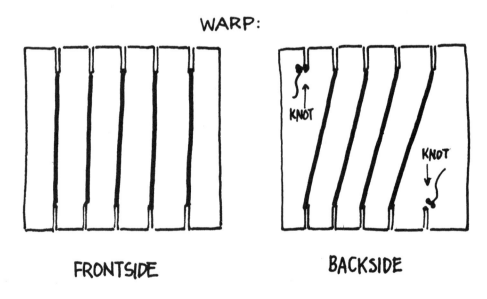

FRONTSIDE   BACKSIDE

Tie a knot to secure the string on the last bottom slot. (The front side will have vertical strings, the back side will have diagonal strings—see illustration.)

The cardloom is now "warped" and you are ready to weave.

Tie a long (36-inch) piece of colored yarn to the bottom left corner warp string, then weave the yarn over the second string, under the third, over the fourth, under the fifth and so on. When you come to the last string in the line at the bottom right corner you will just return (working right to left) in the same alternating fashion. Some children find it easier to go over and under if they have the yarn attached to a large tapestry needle or taped to a tongue depressor. Many children seem to be more comfortable just using their fingers. In either case the results will be the same.

Interesting results can be obtained by changing not only the color of the yarn, but the size. You can also use plastic wrap, tissue paper, or aluminum foil to weave over and under—interspersed with yarn. Beads can be incorporated, strung onto the yarn between over and under.

Comments: These weavings are never removed from the card. The results are always artistic.

God's Eye

(Stick Weaving)

Ages: 5–10 years

Materials & Equipment: 2 (somewhat straight) sticks

Yarn—three or four different colors

Scissors

Directions: Each child needs two sticks that are relatively straight and somewhat equal in diameter and length.

Have children go outside and find sticks. Younger children have an easier time managing heavy, longer (about 12-inch) sticks when they begin the weaving process; older children can make very small, delicate weavings because of their ability to keep the yarn tight and even as they weave.

The two sticks will be bound together in a cross shape. The teacher should do this job for 5- and 6-year-olds, while older children will probably be able to bind the cross themselves. (Directions follow.)

Hold the two sticks at right angles in one hand. Taking a long piece of yarn (36-inch) in the other hand, wrap the yarn tightly on a diagonal where the sticks meet—wrap ten to fifteen times on one diagonal, then cross over and wrap ten to fifteen times on the other diagonal (the sticks should be tightly bound together). See illustration:

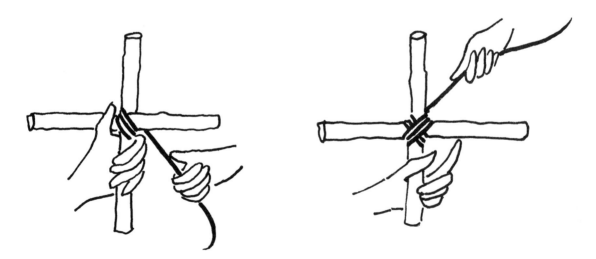

Now you are ready to weave the god's eye. You will have a "loose end" of yarn left after you wrap the diagonals. If it is not at least 24 inches long, attach another piece of yarn of a different color by knotting the ends together (see instructions for weaver's knot on the next page). The cross will be held in one hand, the weaving string in the other. Moving clockwise: wrap over and around the first stick (the closest to your weaving hand) then move clockwise to the next stick and again wrap the yarn over the top, then around, clockwise to next stick, then over and around it. Continue in this fashion, creating a diamond-shaped pattern. Knot on new colors of yarn as the old yarn is used up by the weaving process.

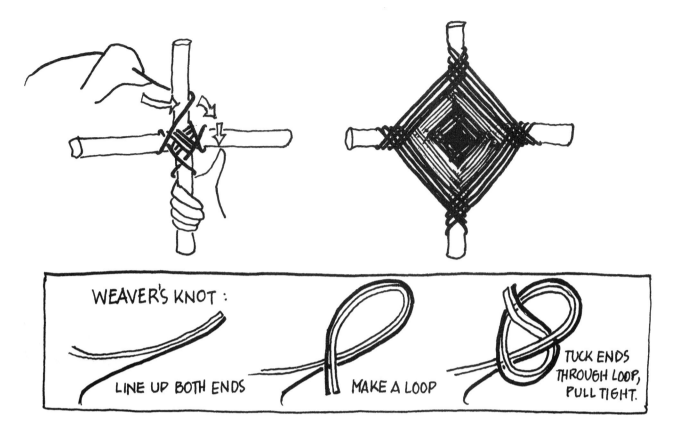

WEAVER'S KNOT :

LINE UP BOTH ENDS

MAKE A LOOP

TUCK ENDS THROUGH LOOP, PULL TIGHT.

Comments: Younger children will wrap the yarn more loosely, and sometimes, reverse directions—the results are still pleasing even though not as "perfect."

At the beginning of learning how to weave from stick to stick, this project requires close attention of the teacher; otherwise, children become confused and frustrated. Plan to do this on a day when you can spend time with each child working at a relaxed pace.

This is a good opportunity for older children to assist younger children in learning a new skill.

Colored Sand

Using colored sand to make designs or pictures on glued paper or contact paper; for outside sand pictures on concrete, earth (dirt), or in the sandbox. Older children can layer the sand in jars, for gifts.

Ages: 3–11 years. Older children will make more sophisticated designs.

Materials & Equipment: White sand will work best. It is available for a small sum at hardware stores. Even brown "river" sand will work well, though colors will be muted.

Coloring agent: Food coloring is preferred and is less messy. But powdered tempera paint or powdered colored chalk can be used.

Jars of various sizes, with lids (See Directions)

Directions: To mix the sand and the coloring, you may use the bowl method or the jar method. First, the bowl method: Using a separate bowl for each color, place about two cups sand in each. To the sand in the bowl, add food coloring, starting with about five drops. Children stir the sand with a wooden spoon or stick. As they stir they watch the color spread from grain to grain. Add more coloring if you want the colors to be darker. Make as many colors as you want. Children could experiment with mixing colors. Cleanup is with soap and water.

The jar method: Fill small jars with lids (baby food jars are best), about two-thirds to three-fourths full with sand, and add a drop or two of food coloring. Replace the lid and shake the jar to distribute the coloring throughout the sand.

Making decorative, layered jars of colored sand:

Children can create a temporary or permanent product by layering different colors of sand into a baby food jar with a spoon. The teacher might demonstrate first. The layers will create wavy stripes. It is necessary to work rather slowly. The teacher should tell the children not to move or shake the jar while working. If children want to keep the product, they should fill the jar with sand to the top, then put on the lid. This will help prevent the sand from undue mixing.

Older children can create more sophisticated art work with larger jars. It is important to allow young children especially, time to experiment. Don't instruct too much how to make a pleasing pattern. Children will learn from each other and by experimentation.

Variations: To create a fancier jar (for children age 7 and up):

1. Once the jar is nearly filled with various stripes, press the point of a pencil or other pointed object down through the sand several times, along the inside edge of the glass. This will make pleasing dips in the stripe. (Sand will move wherever there is a hole.)

2. Or, children can place two or three layers of sand, then punch it (with the pencil); add more layers and punch it. This is another way to create dips in the stripes of sand.

3. Colored sand can be used outside to make pictures on top of dirt or leveled sand in the sandbox. Young children can place handfuls of sand on any level place and draw sticks through the sand to create a pleasing design, or pattern.

4. Pictures or patterns can be "drawn" onto glue-coated paper or the sticky side of contact paper. These are very messy operations, but interesting ones.

Comments: Colored sand art makes a good outdoor activity. In making jars, young children will be satisfied with simple patterns. Older children (7 and up) will become intrigued, will take much more care, and create somewhat more complex designs.

Sand-casting: Medallions or Ornaments

Ages: 5–11 years

**Materials
& Equipment:** A roasting pan, cake pan, or cake pan sized tray, two inches or more in depth; *or* (preferably) cardboard boxes, sometimes called "flats," that grocery stores use to store and display cans of soda. These are 11-by-16-by-2½ inches, and can be thrown away when the project is finished. Readily available at supermarkets.

Wet sand

Plaster of paris, available in bags at hardware stores (*not* Spackle)

Ordinary paper clips, to be used as hooks

Disposable plastic bowls (empty margarine or whipped topping containers)

Directions: Don't have a large group of children working at once, or try to have 15 children finish medallions on the same day. You will need to work with one child at a time, allowing about 20 minutes the first time for each child. Depending on the time available, choose a small group of up to six children to do casting each day. Children can watch each other and learn.

Let's say children are going to make a medallion or ornament to hang around their necks. The first time through should be considered exploratory; children need to get the feel of the process. The first medallion each child makes may need to be discarded. That's typical. The teacher may show a model.

First, fill the flat box with thoroughly damp, but not dripping wet, sand. Sand should be firm and packable, not standing in water. Fill to a depth of 2 to 2½ inches.

The first child makes a mold in the wet sand by making a depression about the size of his/her fist. Make a design with the fingers. Little shells, buttons, gravel, tin foil, may be added to the depression. These will stay permanently in the casting. The hole made by the design can go close to the bottom of the box. The pattern shouldn't be too flat. (Illustration will help to visualize.)

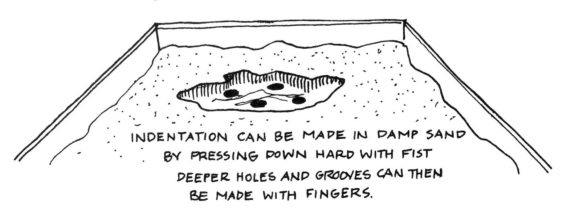

INDENTATION CAN BE MADE IN DAMP SAND
BY PRESSING DOWN HARD WITH FIST
DEEPER HOLES AND GROOVES CAN THEN
BE MADE WITH FINGERS.

Next, mix the plaster. Measure three tablespoons of plaster of paris into a very small container (preferably one you can throw away later). Add all at once, two tablespoons water. Stir. The plaster should be the consistency of heavy cream or thick soup. Work rapidly, as the plaster sets quickly. As soon as it is mixed, carefully pour into the mold in the wet sand.

Adding the hook: After the plaster is poured, immediately place a paper clip into the flat part of the mold so that only about ¼ inch sticks out. Most of the clip will be submerged in the plaster.

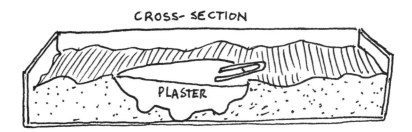

CROSS- SECTION

PLASTER

Remove the casting carefully from the sand after about one hour, and allow it to dry overnight or 24 hours. Next day, brush off the loose sand, and put a heavy string through the paper clip hook so the child can wear the ornament or hang it on his or her locker. Or the class could hang the ornaments on an indoor tree.

Helpful hints: Over a period of days, the sand can be re-used. Six more children can later use the same sand and the same tray, making different molds.

The plaster of paris becomes hot after it's mixed and will slowly cool as it sets. Children can feel the plaster as it cools.

If a sand box is available, the castings can be made there, thus saving a big clean-up. Sand-casting is fun to do outside in the spring.

Because there are chemicals in the plaster, the teacher should make sure the child does not create a dust cloud when spooning out the plaster. **Do not inhale plaster dust.**

Don't mix plaster with the hands. If it gets on the hands, wash it off immediately. Have a bucket of water nearby for this purpose.

Sometimes an older child (8 or 9 years old) can help a younger one.

The castings may be painted with tempera or acrylic paint or water colors.

Sometimes a class makes bird ornaments, then decorates a little tree with them.

Sand-casting: Candles

Ages: 7 years and up

Materials & Equipment: Paraffin (sold in grocery stores with jam-making materials—one package makes two candles—or in hobby shops)

Cardboard "flats" (shallow boxes that are readily available in supermarkets, where they are used to hold cans of soda)

Wet sand to fill the cardboard flat

Candle wicking (inexpensive and available at hobby shop and art supply stores)

2 pound coffee can in which to melt the paraffin

A safe and stable gas or electric stove

Potholders or oven mitts

Directions: **Since this project involves hot wax, safety precautions are paramount: only one child should work at a time, and should be supervised throughout by an adult. Only an adult should pour the hot wax.**

Preparing the mold: Fill the cardboard box with thoroughly moistened (but not drippings wet) sand, to a depth of 2 to 2½ inches. Make a hole using the fist, about 3 or 4 inches across. The hole should be deep and irregular. Put at least four "legs" at the bottom. To make the legs, take a finger and put a long skinny hole on the four "corners" of the larger mold. These "legs" will keep the candle level when it is finished. The holes for the legs need to go to the bottom of the box. The large hole for the candle itself can go to any depth.

Melting the wax: Using one-half package of paraffin for each candle, melt the wax in a 2-pound coffee can set in or over simmering, not boiling, hot water. Melt enough for two candles at one time. Melting takes awhile, usually one hour. Set the mold in a place where it can sit for two days undisturbed while the wax slowly dries and hardens. The mold should not be moved during this time. **Only the teacher should pour the hot wax, holding the coffee can with potholders in both hands.** Coffee can can be discarded.

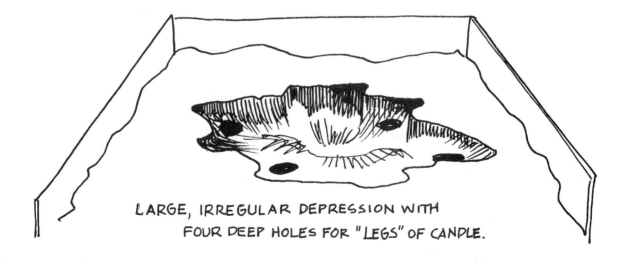

LARGE, IRREGULAR DEPRESSION WITH
FOUR DEEP HOLES FOR "LEGS" OF CANDLE.

Placing the wicks: Tie onto a stick that is long enough to reach across the mold box, enough wicking to go to the depth of the candle. Place the stick so that the wick goes as straight as possible to the bottom center of the candle. Candles may have two or three wicks if you want to get fancy.

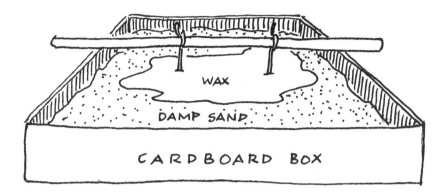

Allow the mold to remain undisturbed until the wax is thoroughly cool and firm. This will take at least two days.

After cooling, lift the candle out of the mold. Brush off excess sand. Cut the wick so that it sticks up one-half inch, and it is ready to use or to give as a gift.

Comments: It is possible to buy candle coloring dye and candle perfume. But these are not necessary. White paraffin makes a very pretty candle and the slightly sandy crust gives the candle an attractive finish.

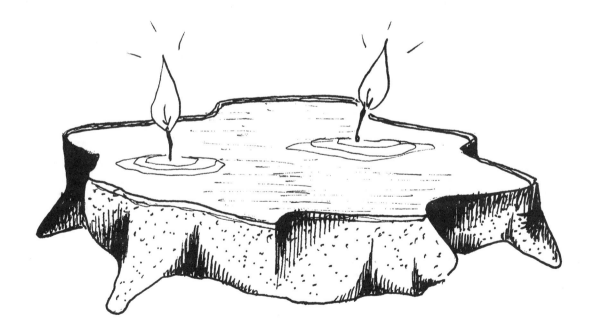

Papier Mâché

Ages: 3 years and up (see comments)

Materials & Equipment:
White glue
Newspaper
Large round balloon
Dishpan or large, flat casserole dish
Smocks

Directions:
Four children for each balloon make a nice, workable group.

Dilute glue: one part glue to two parts water; mix glue in the bottom of the dishpan. To cover a balloon, it will take one large (8 ounce) bottle of glue and two glue containers of water. Children can help with the preparations, especially the newspaper tearing.

Tear newspaper into thin (about ½-inch wide) to medium (1½-inch wide) strips about 6 to 12 inches long. If you tear the newspaper from the top down to the fold, it will tear fairly straight.

Put as many strips into the glue mixture as possible so they will be covered by the solution. Let them soak while you're getting children's smocks on and the balloon inflated and tied tightly.

Cover the table with several layers of newspaper.

Place the inflated balloon in the center of the table and position the children so they can reach it. Place the glue-soaked paper strips where children can reach them, or so the teacher can keep handing them out.

Cover the balloon all over with several layers of strips placed so they will be flat, like tape, with minimum wrinkles. See that there are no gaps in the newspaper cover.

When the balloon is completely covered with the several layers of strips, some glue solution may be left over. Pour this over the balloon, and spread it evenly and gently.

Remove the balloon to a protected place where it can dry undisturbed for 24 to 28 hours. In humid weather, drying takes quite a long time. If you wish to hasten drying time, direct a fan toward the balloon.

After the balloon's cover is thoroughly dry and hard, prick the balloon. Children can then decorate the sphere with strips of colored tissue paper, or it can be painted.

The ball can become the head of an animal or puppet, a piñata, or can be cut in half to make two masks. If it becomes the head of an animal, paper towel tubes can become the four legs, and another tube can be the neck.

See the following activity for making masks and puppets.

Comments: Some 3- or 4-year-olds object to getting their hands sticky and messy. If they don't want to do this activity, don't force the issue.

Instead of a group project with a single large balloon, children could make individual puppet heads (or whatever) using small balloons.

Papier Mâché Puppets or Masks

Ages: 5½–7 years

Materials: See previous pages for making papier mâché puppet heads.

Also needed: Fabric or felt scraps
Yarn and ribbons
Tempera or acrylic paint (not water color)
Glitter
Glue

Directions: *For masks:*

This should be a three-day project.

Cut the papier mâché sphere in half. Cut holes for eyes. Paint the face with tempera in flesh tones of pink, tan or brown, or other colors if desired. Let flesh paint dry overnight before painting eyes, mouth, etc. Decorate with yarn, glitter, ribbons, and fabric scraps. Fasten elastic or rubber bands to the sides.

Variation: Another type of mask can be made by cutting a one-gallon plastic milk carton in half. Cover it well with papier mâché strips. When dry, cut out eye holes and decorate with the materials described above.

For puppets:

After the papier mâché is thoroughly dry and hard, and the balloon has been pricked, there will be a hole in the sphere where the balloon was tied. Into this hole a finger or a cardboard tube (from towels) can be inserted and used as a handle while painting or working on the puppet.

Let the face paint dry thoroughly overnight before painting eyes, mouth, etc. (Making a puppet is a three-day project.)

Glue on yarn for hair, hair ribbons, felt, or fabric for a bandana. A head-band, scarf, or necktie can be added.

Children can use the puppet to tell or read stories to other children. It can be used for dramatic play, or for acting out a skit, simple play or story.

Comments: The puppet will not look like a real human, so older children (ages 8–11) may be disappointed with the results. Therefore, we recommend this type puppet for children 5 through 7.

Slot Puppets

Ages: 3-year-olds enjoy playing with slot puppets but will need assistance making them.

5- to 8-year-olds can make these independently.

Materials & Equipment: Markers or crayons

Scissors

Staple gun

Construction paper

Cardboard strips or popsicle sticks

Directions: Have children draw figures of animals, people, or cars on construction paper. Cut the figures out and staple them to popsicle sticks or cardboard strips, to provide handles for holding puppets.

To make a stage, take a large piece of construction paper and cut a "slot," a straight line close to the bottom of the paper. Lay the stage on a flat surface and stick the handles for the puppets into the slot. The puppets can now be moved along the slot to act out a story.

Scenery may be drawn on the stage if desired.

Comments: Young children also will enjoy playing with the puppets they create, without the slot stage. Older children will enjoy making detailed background scenes for their puppet shows.

If the children seem to need directions, you can suggest making puppets to act out familiar children's stories, such as "The Three Little Pigs."

For very young children, giving the puppets a song to sing, such as "Old MacDonald" or "Did You Ever See A Lassie?" will provide the idea for an entire show.

Sock Puppets

Ages: 3–10 years

**Materials
& Equipment:** Old socks

Glue

Scissors

Assorted "junk," such as felt and fabric scraps, yarn, buttons, pipe cleaners, and tissue paper scraps.

Directions: Give each child an old, clean sock and show children how it fits over your hand to make a moving mouth.

Put glue, fabric scraps, felt, buttons, pipe cleaners, paper scraps, and yarn out on a table. (Younger children might need help figuring out where to begin the face of their puppets.)

Comments: This activity provides children with the opportunity to create a character of their own choosing. Puppets offer many opportunities for imaginative play.

Toothpicks and Marshmallows

Ages: All ages will enjoy this activity.

Younger children will build flat structures, older children and adults may build geodesic domes

Materials: Small marshmallows, round toothpicks, clean cardboard or heavy paper.

Directions: Place miniature marshmallows on one paper plate and toothpicks on another.

Show younger children how the toothpicks are used as building rods Build anything you can imagine. There are infinite possibilities; no two structures will be alike.

Variations: Small drinking straws, plasticene clay, or large raisins also may be used as building materials.

Safety: **The teacher should supervise the use and handling of toothpicks. Discuss safety with children before beginning the project.**

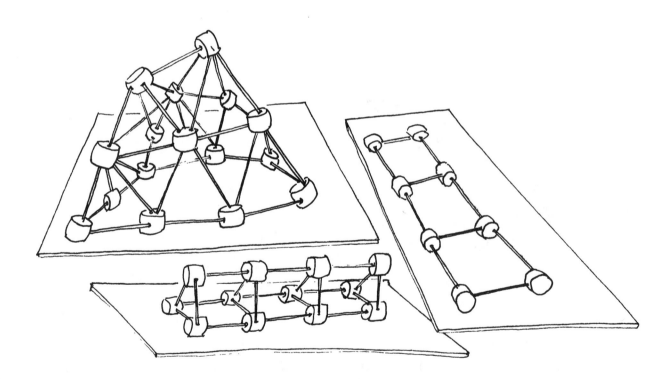

Foam and Pipecleaner Sculptures

Ages: 3–7 years

Materials: Large and small foam packing material

Pipecleaners (chenille strips) cut into different lengths

Foam trays or box lids

Large foam packing pieces may be obtained free from many appliance dealers.

Small round, square and peanut shape pieces can usually be collected from jewelry/china stores. The only costly items for this activity are the pipecleaners.

Directions: Using the larger pieces of foam as a base, children can stick the pipecleaners in the base and twist them into any shape they want. They may wish to add small pieces of foam to the projecting end of the pipecleaner, or add the small pieces to the pipecleaner first. Some children may make realistic figures (people or animals), others may prefer abstract creations. Try to keep the activity open-ended and allow children to experiment with the many ways these pieces can be put together.

Woodscrap Sculpture

Ages: 3–10 years

Materials: Wood scraps (Lumber yards will sometimes offer wood scraps for free. Another source is wood scraps from high school shop classes.)

White glue

Directions: Children will enjoy creating sculptures by gluing together large and small scraps of wood.

There is no way to accomplish this without dripping glue so be sure to use newspaper on the work surface to save yourself difficult clean-up.

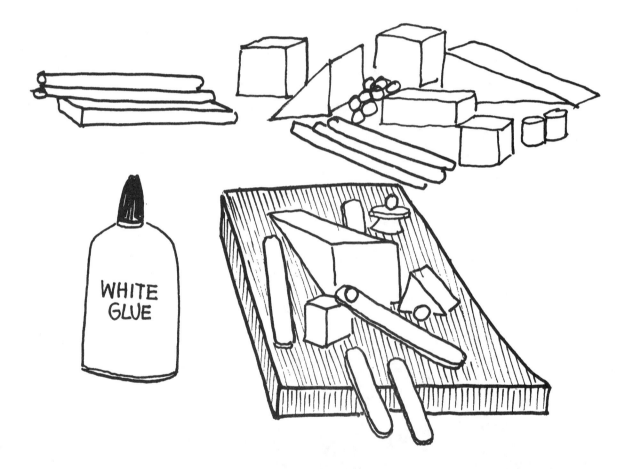

Comments: Children should be gently encouraged to make abstract sculptures rather than recognizable "things": dogs, houses, cars.

Paperbag Building Blocks

(Inexpensive, Reusable Building Material that Children Can Make)

Ages: 3–10 years

Materials: Brown paper grocery bags
Newspaper
Masking tape

Directions: Separate sections of newspaper into single sheets and have children crumple up the paper and stuff it into a grocery bag until the bag is about half full of crumpled paper. Fold top over twice and tape all the way around the bag once.

An assembly line approach works very well if you have at least five to seven children working on this project. Separate children into four work groups:

1. Crumplers
2. Stuffers
3. Folders
4. Tapers

Paper bag blocks are not flat enough to build tall structures but children can use them to build walls if stacked between large cardboard boxes. A group of 5-year-olds built a wonderful castle using this method.

Extended Project: At Hallowe'en time, stuffed grocery bags painted orange make a magnificent pumpkin patch. Tie bags at the top rather than tape to make a stem.

Clay and Play-dough Recipes

Ages: 3 years and up

Materials & Equipment: See recipes

Comments: All of these recipes are comprised of easily available, relatively inexpensive ingredients and produce material to model, pound, and play with. Over the course of the year all should be tried because they are different in texture and quality. No doubt, you will find a favorite that you will mix up time and time again.

Playdough

2½ C. Flour
½ C. Salt
1 T. Alum
1¾ C. Boiling Water
2 T. vegetable oil

OPTIONAL:
* Food coloring or Tempera Powder to color if desired.

Mix flour and salt in a bowl. Mix alum, water oil and food coloring in a separate bowl; add to flour and salt mixture. Knead well. Add extra flour if sticky. No refrigeration is needed. Keep in an airtight container.

Salt dough

1 C. Salt
4 C. Flour
1½ C. Water
4 T. Oil

Mix flour and salt. Add water and oil slowly to the dry ingredients, stirring with a spoon until well blended. Knead dough until soft and pliable. Sculpt objects or use cookie cutters to cut shapes. Bake 45 minutes in 350° oven until hard. Paint with acrylic or varnish to seal.

Silly Putty

1 C. White glue
1½ C. liquid starch

Mix glue and starch in a bowl. You may add a few drops of food coloring if you wish to color the putty. Cover bowl and let stand for a few hours. Pour off extra starch. Knead well. Store in a covered container.

Cornstarch Clay

1 C. Cornstarch
⅓ C. Vegetable oil
⅔ C. Flour

Pour cornstarch* into bowl and add oil. Stir well until syrupy. Gradually add flour until thick and doughy. Knead well. Store in an airtight container.

(*It's fun to play with cornstarch and water– it will not make dough; but the solution is fascinating)

The "original" clay: dirt and water! Find puddle. (children are adept at this!) Dig mud out of bottom with spoons and mix in sandpails.

Mud Pies

1 Puddle
Plastic Sandpails
Spoons
Cookie Sheet

Spoon globs onto cookie sheet. Remove worms. Place in the sunshine until mudpies dry.

Newspaper Rods

Ages: 7–8 years

Materials: Newspaper
Masking tape

Directions: Life-size structures are possible. It is best if four to five children work together taking turns building and rolling newspaper tubes.

Have children roll their own newspaper rods:

1. Place two pieces of newspaper on the floor.
2. Sit at the point of one corner.
3. Fold the corner to the center fold.
4. Beginning at the straight edge, roll the paper as tightly as possible into a tube.
5. Tape the corner to that it won't unroll.

To build:

Use masking tape to connect rods together. The easiest way to begin is to make four or five triangles, then use other rods to connect these together to begin your structure. The strength of the structure will correspond to the strength of each rod. As children become more proficient at rolling, more structures become possible.

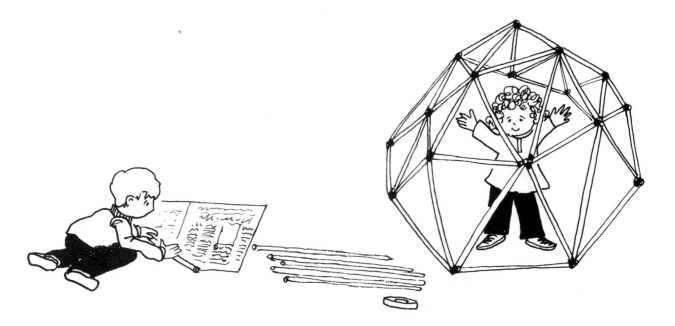

Design Board

Ages: 5–10 years

Materials & Equipment: Wood scraps (2-by-4-inch)
Common nails
Hammer
Colored rubberbands

Directions: Have children hammer nails into a board just far enough for the nails to be secure but leaving enough nail exposed to attach rubber bands.

Nails can be placed in any pattern.

After hammering at least three nails, children attach colored rubber bands in any pattern they choose.

Rubber bands can be changed, added, or removed, so that the child can create many different geometric patterns and use the board over and over again.

Variation: To make a geoboard, nails are hammered in rows one inch apart, with one inch between nails. The geoboard provides mathematical experimentation in addition to eye-hand coordination.

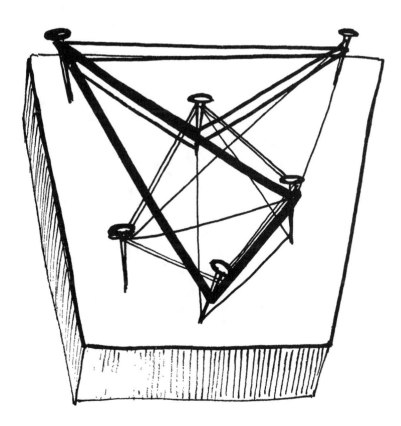

Nail Sculpture

Ages: 4–10 years

Materials & Equipment: A large log, about 8 to 10 inches in diameter, and about 1 or 2 feet long

Two hammers

No. 4 common nails, with heads, available by the pound at hardware stores

Directions: **When preparing to use hammer and nails, take care to position the log in a safe, out-of-the-way place, outside the traffic pattern; a place where the noise will not be disturbing to others and where passers-by won't be accidentally hit.** If possible, place the log on a carpet square or some soft rags, to help muffle the noise.

Hammering is, of course, a good outdoor activity. Indoors, it helps children release excess energy on a very cold or rainy day (or any day).

Young children enjoy hammering nails just for the sake of hammering. Not more than two children should work at one time. Eventually, the project becomes one for the whole group to work on, and it can last for several weeks.

The ultimate goal is to hammer as many nails into the log as possible at whatever angle and depth. The outcome will look something like a porcupine, because most nails will not be hammered all the way into the log. Some children will drive the nail in to a depth of 1 inch, some less, some more.

Comments: The teacher's objective is to provide a safe hammering activity, with little concern for the appearance of the product—though the product will almost certainly end up looking interesting, with its variegated surface of unusual texture.

The project will help develop eye-hand coordination, and will strengthen the small muscles of arm and hand. Children find nail sculpture a calming experience in spite of the noise.

Fringe Cutting

Ages: 3 and 4 years

Materials & Equipment: Scissors with blunt tips

Paper: colored paper scraps, newspaper, newsprint, paper bags

Comments: Children who are learning to use scissors often become fascinated with cutting fringe, and will stay with the activity for a long time. Meanwhile the muscles of the hand are exercised and cutting skills are developed.

Directions: Give children paper that has some body at first. The teacher can draw a few lines on the edge of the paper to get children started, or better, demonstrate. The paper does not have to have a straight edge.

Children can glue some of their fringe frills onto contrasting paper, and create a fringe collage.

Paper Snowflakes

Ages: Easy versions: 4–6 years

More complex versions: up to 10 or 11 years

Materials & Equipment: Only scissors and paper are needed for this entertaining and dexterity-building activity. Drawing paper, typing paper, or newspaper can be used.

Directions: Three or four children can work at one time. By age 6, children can help each other, or older children can help younger ones after they have been through the project a couple of times.

There are two problems children sometimes have when they first start to do fold-and-cut projects:

1. They may not understand what folding means, or they do not press hard enough on the folded edges to make a firm, strong fold. The teacher should demonstrate with a sheet of typing paper how to fold a sheet in half (always using the table as a base) and then in quarters, and how to press with the arm or whole hand to get a firm fold.

2. The other rule that needs explanation involves cutting. The teacher should demonstrate that some places on any folded edge must remain uncut, to hold the finished product in one piece.

Cutting snowflakes:

Using 8½ × 11 typing paper, children fold over in half and hold the paper while rubbing hard along the fold to produce a firm edge. Then fold again into quarters. Children then cut anywhere as long as they leave some part of the fold uncut. It doesn't matter that the paper is oblong. When children begin to understand how the symmetrical patterns are made, they will begin to fold carefully and perhaps progress to more complex folding.

With older children (up through fifth grade, ages 10 or 11), all sorts of variations are possible. They can experiment with different kinds of folds, more folds, creating snowflakes, or making small snowflakes that can then be pasted onto colored paper to make a greeting card.

FOLD & CUT

UNFOLD AND ENJOY!

Paper Doll Chains

Ages: 4–6 years. More complex versions, up to 10 or 11 years.

Materials & Equipment: Scissors

Drawing paper, typing paper, or newspaper

Directions: Start by practicing with a single sheet of typing paper. The teacher should demonstrate first. Fold the typing paper lengthwise into accordion-type pleats (children should see that folding is easiest on the table). The folds should be about 1½ or 2 inches in width. The teacher should draw with pencil, a half a head, an arm, and a leg (half a body, in other words). Make sure the arm extends all the way to the fold. The teacher then cuts along the pencil line, making sure that there is part of the fold (the arm of the doll) that remains uncut. Open up the folded paper, trim off the half doll that remains and staple together with other dolls to make a chain.

Children can experiment with larger paper and more folds (perhaps using newsprint or newspaper) to make longer chains.

Older children can also make heart chains and fourth graders (and up) can, still later (using small embroidery scissors or cuticle scissors) experiment with making white cutout pictures of trees, animals, etc. which they can then paste onto colored paper.

Collage—Three Types

(Nature Collage; Litter Collage; Junk Collage)

Ages: 3–11 years

Materials: *Nature collage:* Natural objects found on a nature walk: e.g., leaves, sticks, grass, seed pods, twigs, feathers; weeds; dry, pressed or uncultivated flowers; gravel, sand, soil; acorns, seeds, pine cones, etc.

Litter collage: Materials collected on a "clean-up" walk: pieces of paper, cellophane, plastic, food wrappers; cans, bottle tops, rubber bands, aluminum tabs, straws, plastic cups, lids; newspapers, plastic bags; anything people have thrown away.

"Clean Junk" collage: Scraps or cuttings of colored or white or tissue paper; egg cartons, aluminum pie plates or foil, buttons, fabric scraps, beads, scraps of yarn, computer paper, dried flowers, interesting pieces of cardboard, etc.

Also: Brown paper bags for collecting

Corrugated cardboard, shirt cardboard, or very heavy stock paper (to prevent curling)

White glue

Directions: Categorize the material you have collected three ways (unless only one type of material is sought).

Assemble objects on a work table where individual cardboards have been laid out, or where one large heavy cardboard is available for several children to work on.

Glue objects down in a way that pleases, generally in an abstract arrangement. Older children may wish to try representational work.

NATURE   LITTER   CLEAN JUNK

Comments: Even young children are surprised by the amount of litter they will find on the sidewalks, in the parks, near their school or center. They will make appropriate observations on the issues of waste disposal and neighborhood ecology.

Parents may be asked to save certain items of clean junk to send to the after-school program.

Related Project: Burying litter (to see what is biodegradable).

Take various samples of the litter and/or nature materials collected and bury them in the ground at a depth of 8 to 12 inches. Make a record and mark the place. Return in three to five weeks, dig up the litter, etc. and see what has dissolved or decomposed and what hasn't. Compare with the record. Children will be surprised to see that cellophane, aluminum, plastic, rubber bands, etc. will remain essentially unchanged. Some metal may have rusted. Organic materials such as newspaper and other paper scraps, grass, flowers, small twigs, etc. will be well on the way to decomposing. Children may not remember the word "biodegradable," but they will not forget the message.

Other organic material (egg shells, banana peels, coffee grounds) may be added to the experiment. Be sure to diagram on paper where each kind of material is buried.

Magazine Collage

Ages: 3–10 years

Materials & Equipment: Old magazines

Scissors

Paste or glue

Construction paper or cardboard

Directions: Magazine collages lend themselves to themes—and the theme can be just about anything. For instance, with younger children, food is a good theme. Have children look through magazines and cut out pictures of food they love. Then paste the pictures onto construction paper to make a food collage.

Animal collages, alphabet collages, car collages, to name a few, are successful with younger children. Older children might enjoy doing a collage about themselves—cutting pictures, advertising slogans, letters and words out of old magazines to make a ME collage.

Solicit old magazines from your student's parents; they are usually delighted to donate them. Ask for a wide variety: *Time, Ladies Home Journal, Life, Ranger Rick, Discovery, Better Homes and Gardens,* mail order catalogues, and *Sports Illustrated,* for example. Collages may present the basics for interesting discussions.

Torn Paper Pictures

Ages: 3–11 years

Materials: Construction paper in different colors
Dark paper (preferably brown or black) for mounting torn shapes
Glue

Comments and Directions: This activity, like many other arts and crafts, can be conducted on many levels, depending on age and ability. It is particularly useful in helping young children, who cannot yet handle scissors well, to see that they can create a satisfying art product with only the fingers as tools. It helps children of all ages to loosen up, to realize that an art creation doesn't have to be "regular" or "realistic" to be artistic. For example, a child might tear a large circle, a small circle, and two tiny ones to create a fanciful mouse, where a "hard-edged" mouse cut with scissors might seem unsatisfying as an end product. A child of first- to fourth-grade age might be frustrated trying to cut a "perfect" circle, but if he or she tears a circle, the unevenness will be acceptable, even pleasing.

Paper tearing often gives children the freedom to lower their perfectionistic expectations. The outcomes are usually quite beautiful, and confidence is developed.

Older children can experiment with both abstract designs and representational pictures (animals, people, houses, etc.).

Torn shapes can be glued to any dark paper (black or brown construction paper, brown wrapping paper, or pieces of corrugated cardboard). Tearing newspaper is an interesting alternative to tearing colored paper.

Sponge Printing

Ages: 3–10 years

Materials: Small flat sponges
Tempera paint or printing ink
Paper plates
Paper

Directions: Cut sponges into a variety of shapes: stars, hearts, triangles, circles, squares.
Mix tempera in small amounts, about the consistency of thick cream, and pour small amounts onto paper plate. Use a separate paper plate for each color. (Paint puddle on plate should not be too deep.)
Wet the sponges in water and wring them out. They should be just damp.
Place each sponge into the tempera then onto paper to print. Combine shapes and colors in whatever fashion you desire.

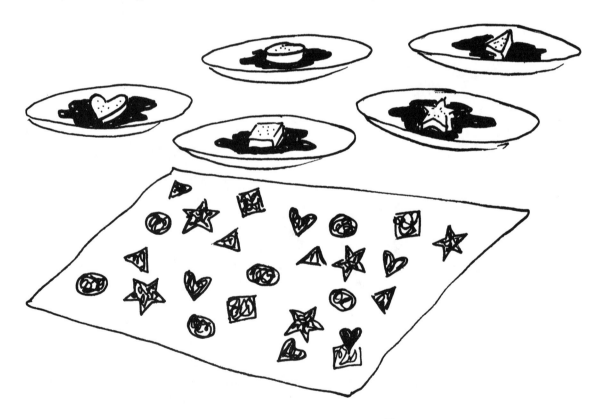

Comments: Older children may want to print some gift wrap paper.

Potato Printing

Ages: 3–11 years

Materials & Equipment: Baking potatoes, or any large size potatoes. Each potato will make two printers.

Knife and spoon

Paper

Color media: paint (tempera or acrylic); printing or India ink; food coloring; stamp pad

Directions: Cut each potato in half horizontally, taking some care to make a flat cut. This will help to ensure a good print.

For young children (ages 3–5) the teacher should carve the design into the cut end of the potato. Older children are fascinated with carving their own designs.

USE SPOON TO "DIG" CIRCULAR HOLES

USE KNIFE TO MAKE STRAIGHT CUTS

Designs are made by removing pieces of potato, where you don't want an ink image. This is called a relief print. What you cut away will not print. Cuts do not have to be deep (see illustration).

After the design is cut into the potato, any color media is placed on a dish, plastic lid, or flat pan. Only enough paint is needed to cover the flat surface of the potato. After it is dipped, the potato is carefully pressed onto paper.

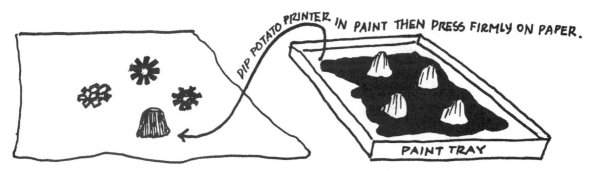

DIP POTATO PRINTER IN PAINT THEN PRESS FIRMLY ON PAPER.

PAINT TRAY

Variations & Comments: An obvious advantage to potato printing is that many copies can be made. Potato designs can be used for decorating greeting cards, invitations, note paper. To make gift wrapping paper, use the potato print over and over on tissue or other large paper.

Snowflake designs may be made in winter, flower shapes in spring. Some teachers object to using food in arts and crafts work. Flat sponges, cut with scissors into shapes, may be used instead of potatoes.

Monoprinting

Ages: 4–11 years

Materials & Equipment: Water-base printing ink, available at art supply stores. Other types of color media do not work as well. Only one color is necessary, though a variety may be used.

Brayer (roller)

Paper: typing or drawing paper, or any type, even newspaper, about 8½ by 11 inches in size

Window glass: a small pane about 5" × 7"

Various objects with which to scratch a design, such as a comb, paper clips, or fork

Bucket of water, paper, and towels

Smocks

Directions: One child at a time works with the printing equipment. If there is a second pane of glass, two children can work simultaneously. A small amount of printing ink is squeezed onto the glass. The brayer (roller) is then used to spread the ink so as to cover the glass completely. If the ink does not cover, a small additional amount of ink can be squeezed onto the glass.

Next, the child scratches a design into the layer of printing ink, with a fork, comb, or other object. A piece of 8½-by-11-inch paper is then centered over the paint-covered glass, the paper is lowered onto the paint, and the back side of the paper is rubbed gently with a fingertip. Lift the paper carefully off the glass and you will have a one-of-a-kind print. After each print, wash the glass in a bucket of water and dry it with a paper towel.

LIFTING PRINT OFF

← INK COATED GLASS WITH DESIGN SCRATCHED IN

BRAYER

Comments: This art product makes a pleasing gift that parents often want to frame. Too much ink on the glass will obliterate the design. A smeared print may indicate too much ink was used.

Styrofoam Printing

Ages: 5–10 years

Materials & Equipment:
Styrofoam meat trays
Pencil
Water-base printing ink
Roller or brayer
Paper

Directions: Give each child a meat tray and pencil. Turn the tray upside down and use a pencil to draw a picture on the bottom of the tray. The styrofoam is soft and the pencil will make a dark line and indent the styrofoam.

Squeeze ink onto a paper plate and roll brayer in ink until it is covered with ink, then roll the brayer over the design on the bottom of the meat tray.

Turn meat tray over onto a clean sheet of paper and rub and press with the fingers, being careful not to move the meat tray around.

Lift the meat tray carefully off the paper. Set the print aside to dry.

2

INDOOR and OUTDOOR GAMES

Children need some physical activity after a day of mostly sedentary school work. Vigorous games, in which every child can succeed, are more than an energy outlet. They help develop gross and fine motor skills, social skills, body awareness, and self-confidence.

Many games labeled "indoor games" can also be played outdoors and vice versa. Most of the games in this section can be played in small groups or with just one friend. Some (such as ball bouncing or rope jumping) can be enjoyed individually. Other games (such as Beanbag Shuffleboard or Beanbag Bowling) can be played three ways: alone, with a friend, or in a small group.

It is important to keep introducing new games. Don't overdo the same old favorites. Each new game is like a puzzle—or a problem to be solved. It is when an activity is new that children extend themselves. This is when they learn the most about themselves and about the rules, style, and the point of a game. Of course, they also learn new physical skills. Please encourage all your quiet children to participate, at least part of the time, in active games if at all possible. See also pages 217–223 for card games.

Bouncing Ball

Ages: 5–12 years

Benefits: Children develop mental concentration and physical coordination.

Equipment: Chalk to draw a court on sidewalk or blacktop
A large rubber ball that bounces well

Directions: A court of eight squares is drawn, onto which a ball may be bounced, as suggested. The court may consist of one or two rows of numbers.

Children should practice bouncing the ball continuously in each of the eight squares first.

The first child bounces the ball consecutively in each of the eight squares while naming eight girls' names. If he or she succeeds, he starts the bounces again in each square while naming eight boys' names. Repeat the action in the following sequences:

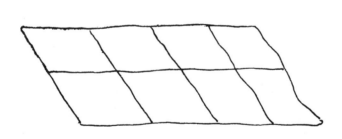

Girls' names
Boys' names
Teachers' names
Street names
Color names
Car names
Countries' names
States' names

Of course, any category can be substituted for the above categories.

Animals, fruits, vegetables, rivers, presidents, multiplication tables, Indian tribes, oceans, baseball teams, famous women, months; when a child misses, his or her turn is ended.

What constitutes a miss: unable to name continuously, unable to bounce ball continuously, bouncing outside the square. Start from where you missed.

Comments: Any agreed-upon rules may be used to make the game easier or harder. For example, a younger group might bounce and catch the ball each time instead of dribbling it, or might bounce the ball in *one* square instead of eight, or you could enlarge the size of the squares.

Wall Ball

Ages: 6 years and up

Materials & Equipment: A tennis ball or a small hard rubber ball that bounces well is used in this activity.

Find a wall against which to throw the ball and a fairly hard, smooth surface on which the ball can bounce.

Directions: A child can play this game individually, with a partner, or in a small group.

1. Throw ball at wall, let it bounce once and catch it.
2. Throw ball at wall and without a bounce, catch it.
3. Throw ball at wall, let it bounce once, clap hands, catch ball.
4. Throw ball at wall (without a bounce), clap hands, and catch it.
5. Throw ball under right leg and hit the wall, let it bounce, and catch it.
6. Throw ball under left leg, and hit the wall, let it bounce, and catch it.
7. Throw ball under right leg and hit the wall (no bounce), clap hands, and catch it.
8. Throw ball under left leg and hit the wall (no bounce), clap hands and catch it.
9. Throw the ball at wall, turn around as it bounces, and then catch it.
10. Throw the ball at wall, turn around and catch it. (no bounce)
11. Throw the ball at the wall, turn around as it bounces, clap hands and catch it.
12. Throw the ball at the wall, turn around, clap hands and catch it (no bounce).

Comments: When you can perform all these patterns without a mistake, try clapping twice every time there is a clap hands part in the pattern. The next time try clapping *three* times—all before you catch the ball. Remember, the ball can never bounce more than once and in some parts of the pattern it does not bounce at all.

This is an old and still popular street or playground activity. Perhaps some people will remember the "thump thump" sound on the sides of their houses.

Bounce and Bounce

Rita Shotwell

Ages: 8 years and up

Benefits: Coordination
Concentration
Motor skills
Auditory skills
Group cooperation

Equipment: Ball

Directions: Children stand in a circle. One child starts bouncing a ball and saying the rhyme while bouncing.

On the word "pass," the child bounces the ball to the person on the right and that person continues bouncing, and starts the rhyme over again.

Rhyme:
                    Bounce and bounce and bounce all day,
                    Bounce and bounce and *pass* this way.

Variation 1: Try bouncing the ball and saying the rhyme very fast.

Variation 2: Bounce the ball and say the rhyme very slowly.

Variation 3: Start bouncing slow and gradually get faster and faster.

Comments: This activity can be done with as few as two children.

One, Two, Three O'Leary

Ages: 8 years and up

Benefits: Coordination
Concentration
Motor skills

Equipment: Balls (one for each child if possible)

Directions: Practice bouncing the ball to a steady beat while saying the following rhyme (or the verse can be sung to the tune of "Ten Little Indians"):

> One, two, three O'Leary
> My first name is Mary
> If you think it's necessary
> Look it up in the dictionary.

Each line of the rhyme has four beats, indicated by the underlines. As the child says each line, he bounces the ball on each of the first three beats. Then, on the fourth beat, he swings his right leg up and over the ball without touching. Catch the ball on the last beat of the last line.

The child repeats the verse, this time with the left leg over the ball.

During the third time through, the child forms a large circle with hands and arms and allows the ball to bounce up through the arms on the last word of each line. Other tasks, such as turning around, may be added.

Comments: Once the rhyme and tasks are learned "down pat," the child may try speeding up the rhyme faster and faster without making a mistake.

Traditional verse:

> One, two, three, O'Leary
> Four, five, six, O'Leary
> Seven, eight, nine, O'Leary
> Ten, O'Leary Postman.

Jump Rope Chants and Activities

Ages: 6 years and up

CINDERELLA

Equipment: This jump rope activity can be done with children using individual ropes, or, a big rope is swung by two children and everyone takes turns.

Directions: The idea is to see how many times you can jump before you make an error.

Rhyme:

Cinderella, dressed in yellow,
Went upstairs to kiss a fellow,
By mistake she kissed a snake,
How many doctors did it take?
1, 2, 3, – – – – – – – – –

Variation: Another even sillier version:

Cinderella, dressed in yellow,
Went upstairs to kiss a fellow,
On the way her girdle busted,
How many people were disgusted?
1, 2, 3, – – – – – – – – –

TEDDY BEAR

Directions: The challenge in this activity is to add motions while you continue to jump. It takes some skill to "touch the ground," "turn around," and "pat your thigh" without losing the rhythm of jumping.

Rhyme:

Teddy bear, teddy bear, touch the ground,
Teddy bear, teddy bear, turn around,
Teddy bear, teddy bear, jump real high,
Teddy bear, teddy bear, pat your thigh.

Variation:

The last line of the chant lends itself to different endings such as:

- touch the sky (reach both hands up)
- wave bye bye (and jump out)

DOWN IN THE VALLEY

Directions: Again, the challenge is to see how many times the jumper can jump before missing.

Also, in this chant children have the opportunity to use their friend's names at appropriate spots.

Rhyme:

Down in the valley where the green grass grows,
There sat (someone's name) sweet as a rose,
She/he sang, she/he sang, she/he sang so sweet,
Along came (someone's name) and kissed her/him on the cheek.
How many kisses did he/she give him/her?
1, 2, 3, – – – – – – – – –

I WAS BORN IN A FRYING PAN

Directions: This is another test of how long one can continue to jump. The task can be made more difficult by hopping only on one foot during the counting part.

Rhyme:

I was born in a frying pan,
I was born in a frying pan,
Can you guess how old I am?
1, 2, 3, – – – – – – – – –

FIRST AND SECOND GRADE

Directions: Each child jumps in while the rope is turning. The first time, the child jumps one time ("first grade") and then jumps out. The second time, the child jumps two times ("second grade") and then jumps out, and so on.

The object of this game is to see what grade you can get to. Children continue to chant the grade in order to remember the number of times to jump.

Jumping in and out of a turning rope takes some practice. Having more than one child do it at one time makes the challenge even greater.

Bobby Bear

Rita Shotwell

Ages: 6–9 years

Benefits: Eye-hand coordination
Social interaction

Directions: Tap a steady beat, on different parts of the body while saying the rhyme so children will become familiar with the words. (Tap head, shoulders, thighs, knees, feet, elbows, etc.)

After children learn the words, have everyone take a partner and do a simple hand clapping pattern with their partner, while saying the rhyme. It's fun to go a little faster each time you repeat the rhyme.

Code:

O = clap own hands
R = clap partner's right hand
L = clap partner's left hand

Rhyme:

Bobby Bear was dancing a-long,
O   R   O   L

Kicking his toes and singing a song,
O   R   O   L

Along came Michelle with a smile so sweet,
O   R   O   L

Jumped up and down and kissed him on the cheek!
O   R   O   L

Variation 1:

For younger children, omit the hand clapping part and only tap a steady beat on body parts.

Variation 2:

Can also be used as a jump rope rhyme. Each child should have his or her own rope or do as a group activity with two children holding the rope and one child jumping until the words, "along came Michelle," then another child will jump in and both will jump until the end of the rhyme. First child jumping can then jump out at the end and game will start over again.

Mabel Able

(Jump Rope Activity)

Ages: 6 years and up

Directions: Chant:

> Mabel Able set the table
> Don't forget the salt and pepper
> Salt and pepper, salt and pepper, salt and pepper, etc.

The person jumping continues to jump as long as possible as the other children chant "salt and pepper" over and over again. When the jumper stops, the word she/he stops on is noted and the children turning the rope react immediately. If the word stopped on is "salt," the rope is turned slowly as the jumper begins jumping again; if the word is pepper, the rope is turned very fast, until the jumper misses.

Variation: If the jumper stops on "salt," she/he must jump crossing her/his feet alternately each time.

Rock 'N' Roll Kid

Rita Shotwell

Ages: 8 years and up

Benefits: Motor skills
Auditory skills
Coordination
Group cooperation

Equipment: Jump rope
Ball (for variation)

Directions: The teacher says the rhyme several times so children can learn the words.

Rhyme:

> I'm a rock 'n' roll kid with dancin' feet,
> A movin' and a groovin' to a steady beat.
> I snap my fingers and tap my toes,
> I turn my body and touch my nose.

After children learn the rhyme, they may walk, to a steady beat, while saying the rhyme. They follow the directions of the words on the last two lines:

> I snap my fingers and tap my toes,
> I turn my body and touch my nose.

Variation 1: Jump rope game:

Two children turn a long rope. Other children take turns jumping in one at a time, while saying the rhyme and doing the actions.

Variation 2: Ball bouncing game:

Try bouncing a ball while saying the rhyme and doing the actions. A large ball will be easier. The hardest part will be to turn around fast enough to hit the ball and continue with the bouncing.

Tiger Ball

Ages: 2–4 years

Benefits: Attention building (tracking the ball)
Listening for a signal
Social give and take
Eye-hand coordination

Equipment: A large ball

Directions: Children sit in a circle (a small circle of five to eight children provides more learning opportunity). If the group is large, divide into two or three circles. Children chant the following verse:

Tiger ball, tiger ball,

Where it stops, no one knows.

If you're caught holding it,

You become a tiger.

On the word, "Tiger," whoever is holding the ball at that moment must lose a turn, and sit in the center of the circle. Children do not mind this penalty in the slightest because they are the center of attention and because their time out is very brief.

Comments: This game, while very, very simple, is a great delight for little children. It teaches them, in the gentlest way, something about cooperation through simple give and take.

Beanbag Bowling

Ages: 3–11 years

Equipment: One or two beanbags
Four or more Pringle™ cans
The game requires a smooth, shiny floor to play on.

Benefits: Eye-hand coordination
Relaxation

Directions: Arrange Pringle™ cans any way you like. We suggest arranging four cans in a diamond shape. The "shooter" throws and slides the beanbag to try to knock down as many "pins" as possible. After two throws, the "shooter" becomes the "pin setter" and sets up the Pringle™ cans for the next bowler.

Older children may want to use more "pins" or set them at a greater distance from the throw line. Older children may also want to learn "real" scoring.

Comments: This is a game a child can play alone or in a very small group. A roll of plastic carpet cover (runner) could be used as a bowling alley if no slippery floors are available. There is something very satisfying about sliding a beanbag across the floor and watching it plow into a line of pins. Children learn to increase the force of their throwing while maintaining aim.

Beanbag Shuffleboard

Ages:　6–12 years

Benefits:　Eye-hand coordination
Balance using a pole
Aim
Understanding principles of force and speed

Equipment:　At least one beanbag for two children
A broomstick may be used as a variation (see below).

Directions:　Paint, draw, or mark with masking tape, one shuffleboard court onto a smooth, shiny floor surface.
The triangular courts should be large to permit easy scoring.

Children take turns (two tries per turn) trying to land a beanbag on one of the numbers.

Scoring should be simple; three points for the most difficult "square," two points for middle squares, one point for the most numerous or largest squares on the court.

Variations:

One child can play alone and can add up the score for five (or any number) throws. Or a child can just continue to throw to increase skill at aiming.

Two children—each has own beanbag—in direct competition: each throws one bag to see who gets highest score. Two children can also play a cumulative score—who has highest score after five throws (children must be old enough to add numbers after each turn).

A broomstick may be used as a shuffleboard stick.

Balloon Badminton

Ages: 3½–10 or 12 years

Benefits: Visual tracking
Eye-hand coordination
Balance
Relaxation

Equipment: A round balloon for each child; the larger the balloon, the easier it is to follow and hit.
Racquets or paddles are desirable but not necessary.

Directions: The balloon may be struck with the open palm. However, a racquet requires a slightly different kind of coordination skill and is more fun.
A racquet may be constructed in a few minutes by second graders (7 or 8 year olds) as follows:

1. Pull a wire coathanger into a diamond shape.

2. Stretch the foot of an old nylon stocking over the wire frame.
3. Fasten the fabric to the neck of the coathanger with a wire tie.
4. **Bend the hook of the coathanger into the neck so there is no sharp edge exposed.** This makes the handle.

Comments: By batting the balloon back and forth across a rope or string line on the floor, children can play a game of "badminton" or "volleyball." It's more fun if no score is kept.

Pom-Pom Paddle Ball

Ages: 7–11 years

Benefits: Visual tracking
Eye-hand coordination
Balance

Equipment: *To make the pom-poms:*

Yarn

6-inch square pieces of cardboard

To make the paddles:

4- to 5-inch lengths of broom handle
Coathangers that are bent into a diamond shape
Nylon stockings
Glue

Directions: Pom-poms are made by looping yarn around a 6-inch piece of cardboard until yarn can form a small ball. Slip the yarn loops off the cardboard and secure in the middle with a knotted piece of yarn. Clip the ends of the loop and shape the pom-pom to be fairly round.

The paddle may be made by drilling a hole into one end of a piece of broom handle. Bend the wire hanger into a diamond shape, cut off the hook with a pair of pliers and place the wire ends into the hole of the broom handle piece. Glue thoroughly. Stretch a section of nylon stocking over the wire frame to form a paddle or racket.

Hit the pom-pom back and forth between two partners, with or without keeping score.

Freddie the Frog

Rita Shotwell

Ages: 4–6 years

Benefits: Eye-hand coordination
Motor skills: grasping, releasing, and throwing
Spatial awareness: distance from beanbag to box

Equipment: Beanbag and box

Chant:

> Freddie the Frog went to jump on a log
> And, <u>SPLASH</u>, he fell into the pond.

Directions: Can be done standing or sitting. Put a box in the center of a small circle of children. Give one child the beanbag. Everyone says the chant while the child with the beanbag throws it from one hand to the other while chanting. On the word "splash," the child throws the beanbag into the box in the center of the circle. Keep repeating the chant until everyone has a chance with the beanbag.

  If there is a large group of children, have several small circles with one beanbag per circle.

Jump Over the Brook

Ages: 4–10 years (all these ages mixed)

Benefits: Space judging
Leg strengthening
Motor skills
Self-testing

Directions & Equipment: Two moderately long ropes (twine would do) are spread on the floor so that they are close together at one end (15 inches apart) and fairly far apart at the other end. The space between the ropes is called the "brook." Children line up and one by one they attempt to jump across the ropes at any point that they want. If they are successful, they may try the brook at a wider point on their next turn.

Children should be warned that younger and smaller children should not be expected to jump as far as older or taller ones.

The teacher may measure the distance jumped by various children or have the older children do this with a yardstick. A simple record could be kept of each child's best jumping distance, then, in a few days or weeks, see if children can match or improve their own earlier records.

Comments: The teacher can add, "Don't get your feet wet."

Back to Back

Ages: 5–10 years

Benefits: Body awareness

Quick thinking and creative problem solving

The game is a good icebreaker or get-acquainted activity.

Directions: The teacher divides the children into pairs and each pair stands back to back. In this game, children (in pairs) must find a way to stand close together, with, for example, one child's elbow touching the partner's elbow, *and* one child's knee touching the partner's knee. There are several ways the problem could be solved.

BACK TO BACK   ELBOW TO KNEE

After children figure a way, the teacher says, "Back to Back." This is the signal to quickly find a new partner and stand back to back with him or her. The teacher gives another problem—such as, "Touch waist to waist and toe to toe." As soon as children solve the problem, the teacher says, "Back to Back"; children change, find another partner, and stand back to back ready to solve a third problem.

Depending on the age of the children, the body problems can be very easy or very difficult.

Variation: (This can be sung to the tune of "Skip To My Lou")

> Head to head and knee to knee,
> I'll touch you and you touch me,
> Find a partner, look around,
> Back to back, don't make a sound.
>
> Wrist to wrist and toe to toe,
> Try to walk, away we go.
> Find a partner, look around,
> Back to back, don't make a sound.
>
> Ankle, ankle, hand to ear,
> Touch me gently never fear.
> Find a partner, look around,
> Back to back, don't make a sound.
>
> —Lynn Davis

Comments: Don't have children pick their own partners to start the game. It leads to quibbling. Once the game has started, children will find a new partner close at hand.

The game should move quickly to keep interest up.

Five Obstacle Course "Carnivals"

Ages: 6 years and up

Benefits: Variety of motor skills
Noncompetitive social skills

Equipment: Varied; see directions

Comments: An obstacle course, especially when newly set up, is like a carnival to children, intriguing and satisfying. Courses may be arranged using large permanent playground equipment, or using the simplest of indoor supplies: beanbags, hoops, ropes, boxes, string, homemade picture cards, chairs. Even the simplest obstacle course need never be boring.

Directions: At its simplest, an obstacle course is an arrangement of tasks, usually using simple equipment, laid out in a circle or circuit. Or, you could call it a series of stations arranged so that several of the stations may be used simultaneously, each by an individual child. Each child stays at one station for a few minutes, working at the task that is presented there. For example, one task might be bouncing a ball continuously with the nonpreferred hand. A second station may consist of a mat and a large wooden box, where a child jumps from a certain height. At a third station, the child might perform a series of somersaults, and a fourth station might require a child to walk backwards on a balance beam. Each child who is participating moves through all stations either at her/his own speed, or at time intervals decided by the teacher—say, five minutes at each station. Six or seven stations complete the circuit.

At the beginning, show those children who will be participating how to use any equipment, toys, tools, etc. contained in the course. Specify how much time the children will be allowed at each station. Tell the children they may be interrupted before they are entirely finished with the task, but that this carnival is for "tasting," i.e. for trying a variety of activities in a short time. Later, children should be allowed to go back to any or all stations and have unlimited turns.

Equipment should be chosen that is safe, challenging but not frustrating, and not easily damaged; something the child can use with a minimum of help.

The following are some examples of obstacle courses that require a minimum of expensive equipment. Of course, you need not be limited by these suggestions. Perhaps you have other equipment you can improvise with.

1. *Large Equipment Obstacle Course* might include: a jungle gym or other climbing equipment; a wooden packing box from which to jump onto a mat; a ladder lying flat to jump or hop through; a knotted heavy rope to swing on or climb; balance beams at various heights; a series of rubber tires to jump in and out of or to crawl through; a tunnel made of tables, cardboard cartons, and/or an old bedspread.

2. *Walking-Jumping Obstacle Course* using: cardboard footprints taped to the floor in a variety of jumping and hopping patterns; numbers and letters also taped to the floor, twisted into various jumping or hopping patterns; hula hoops laid flat to jump through; rope or twine draped between chairs for jumping over; ropes or masking tape arranged in various ways to walk on or beside, or frontwards, backwards, sideways, between, across, or with crossover steps, etc.

3. *Easy Calisthenics Course:* The teacher may spread several mats or rugs on the floor, each a station for a certain easy exercise. Each station should be marked by a stick-figure picture. Exercises might include sit-ups, push-ups, leg lifts, arm circles, knee-bends, toe-touches, etc. At some stations, there might be both an easy and a hard version of the exercise, from which the child may make a choice. The demands should be well within the child's capability. This course should have a short but happy life.

Yoga postures could also be used, and since these have interesting names, interest may be quickly captured. Any library will have a picture book of easy yoga postures. Some of the easy ones include: the tripod head stand, the plough, the cobra, the candle.

Ideally the teacher should supervise this type of obstacle course fairly closely. Calisthenics can be boring unless there's a cheering section.

4. *Object-Handling Obstacle Course:* A lot of beanbags, Nerf™ balls, light plastic balls, or yarn balls, are needed for this course. Stations might include any of the following:

a. Toss beanbags into a basket or tray placed 8 to 10 feet away from a starting line. Retrieve beanbags, replace them, and progress to the next station.

b. Throw beanbags at a large target, such as three hoola hoops lined up flat on the floor as a triangle. Retrieve and replace before moving on.

c. Throw beanbags (or other safe objects) into one or more large boxes, or onto a clean metal garbage can lid, while standing on a small platform or balance beam. Retrieve, etc.

d. Hit a hanging wiffle ball with a plastic bat, as hard as you can. **(Arrange for safety so that passers-by will not be hit accidentally.)**

e. Toss pennies into metal pie plates from a distance.

f. Drop a table tennis ball with the left hand onto a flat surface (table), let it bounce once or more and catch it with a pie tin or plastic bowl held in the right hand.

g. Throw a Nerf™ ball or beanbag at a clown or other target (flat or upright).

h. Try to hit a large target with a sailing paper plate or sponge Frisbee™.

5. *A Fine-Motor Obstacle Course Carnival:* While fine motor activities or tasks are not usually thought of as parts of an obstacle course, they can make a delightful "carnival" while giving children practice in various eye–hand coordination skills. Arrange any of the suggested equipment in a circuit, using tables and chairs, and/or mats on the floor. Of course the circuit doesn't have to be a circle—any arrangement will do as long as children understand in which direction they must move to get to the next station.

a. A plastic stencil with paper and pencil, that may be used in either a conventional or a creative way

b. A large chalkboard that may be drawn on with 2 × 2 inch chunks of damp kitchen sponge

c. A sand tray, in which the child can print or draw using a finger or an old ball point pen

d. A geo-board with new rubber bands, string, or new designs (see page 35)

e. An old deck of cards with which to build a card house, or with which to practice shuffling

f. A magnifying glass and "fresh," nonfragile objects to look at: pine cones, cloth, dried flowers, newspaper, etc

g. A magnifying mirror or mirrors

h. Magnets and a variety of small steel objects

i. Design blocks with new, easy designs that children can arrange the blocks *on,* if they wish

j. Clowns or nonsymmetrical blocks, with which to build a tower

k. Punch-out designs: With a safe stylus such as an old ball point pen, children can punch designs into styrofoam meat trays, or onto paper laid on a carpet square

l. Coin-rubbings (paper, pencil and a variety of coins or similar flat objects)

SIT~UPS
(DO ONE OR MORE)

HARD   NOT-SO-HARD

FROG HEAD STAND
(KNEES BALANCE ON ELBOWS)

(COUNT TO 10)

CANDLE (SHOULDER STAND)

(COUNT TO 30)

COBRA

(COUNT TO 25)

PLOUGH

(COUNT TO 25)

YOGA CARNIVAL PICTURES

Blind Man's Bluff

Ages: 6–10 years

Benefits: Sharpens listening and tactile skills

Equipment: A bandana or other blindfold
A long rope or length of twine, if desired

Directions: Mark off a large circle or square (10 feet diameter or 10 feet square). The circle can be larger or smaller depending on the number of children playing. The more children, the larger the "field." The first "It" will be blindfolded, using a bandana (a bandana is hard to see through, peek under, and it doesn't slip). The other children find a place within the field from which they can move one foot, bend over, or crouch down, but they must keep one foot on their chosen spot. The Blind Man or Blind Lady moves around trying to find a friend. The friend tries to elude "It" by bending, stretching, or stooping. When the "Blind Person" finds someone, he tries to guess who it is by patting the friend's clothing, hair, etc. Technically, if the Blind Person cannot guess who the friend is, he or she must keep on searching. But more children will have a chance for a turn being the Blind Man, if the turn passes each time the Blind Man guesses. No one should get two turns until everyone has had one.

The teacher guides the "Blind Man" if he or she wanders away from the circle.

Variation:

In a game called "Marco Polo," the Blind Person ("It"), may call "Marco" and whichever child is closest to "It" must answer "Polo." This gives "It" some auditory clues.

Comments: The game may be made easier by using a smaller area for the field; it may be made harder for older children by expanding the field. A clothesline rope may be used to define the boundaries.

Human Machine

Ages: 7 years and up

Benefits: Coordinating sounds with actions
Social Skills (working with a partner)

Equipment: Assorted rhythm and percussion instruments (for variation)

Directions: Tell the children to close their eyes and pretend there is a great big machine in the middle of the room. The machine has many small moving parts, and each part has its own sound. As the part moves, it is accompanied by the sound.

With eyes still closed, have children start to make sounds with their mouths, and move their bodies or a part of the body to accompany the sound. (They are to pretend they are part of this big machine.)

When the children feel comfortable moving to the sounds, have them open their eyes so they can see everyone else. Give them a minute or two to enjoy other children's movements, then give them a signal to stop.

Variation 1:

Children stand around the sides of the room. Have them decide what sound and movement they will make to form the human machine.

One child goes to the center of the room and starts his or her sound and movement. One by one, the rest of the children go to the center and join in. (They must link onto each other in some way: touch shoulders, knees, toes, or have one hand or even one finger touch someone to "link" on to the human machine.)

When all have joined in, let them continue for a minute or two and then give a signal to stop.

Variation 2:

Have an assortment of rhythm and percussion instruments on hand: tambourine, hand drum, maracas, finger cymbals, bells, etc.

Children will each have a partner and each pair will select one instrument. One child will play the instrument and the partner will move to the sound. After each set of partners decides on an instrument and a movement, start the human machine going.

Children with instruments stay at the side of the room. Only the partner goes into the center to help form the machine. The instrument players have to watch their partners so the sound will correspond to their partners' movement.

Ping-Pong Balls and Potato Chip Cans

Ages: 8 years and up

Equipment: A Ping-Pong ball and can for each child participating

Benefits: Eye–hand, eye–body coordination
Visual tracking of fast-moving object
Balance and general coordination

Directions: A child or children of older ages can have a wonderful, relaxing time, while sharpening visual tracking skills, by being turned loose in a large room with a Ping-Pong ball and a Pringle™ can.

Younger children, and perhaps older ones too, need no rules. The object is to release the ball with one hand, let it bounce once or more, and catch it with the other hand holding the can. Older children might want to play a game, alone or with a friend, where they try to catch the ball after one bounce, two bounces, three bounces, etc.

It requires considerable skill to coordinate hand, eye, and body in order to catch the elusive little ball.

For younger children or those for whom this activity is difficult, use a wider-mouthed container, such as a peach or coffee can.

The Ping-Pong ball makes a satisfying "klunk" when it's caught in a metal or cardboard container.

The cans may be decorated with spray paint or wrapped with self-adhesive contact paper, as a craft project.

Variations on "Skip to My Lou"

Ages: 3–5 years

Directions & Comments: Children will sing and move around the room freely, but all follow a single locomotion pattern, which the teacher or a leader changes with each verse. This activity provides vigorous indoor exercise on a rainy day, as well as fun and certain social skills. It also works on coordination and control: stopping, starting, and changing.

SKIP, SKIP, SKIP TO MY LOU; SKIP, SKIP SKIP TO MY LOU

SKIP, SKIP, SKIP TO MY LOU; SKIP TO MY LOU, MY DAR-LING.

Variations:

Jump, jump, jump to my Lou, etc.
Hop, hop, hop to my Lou, etc.
Fly, fly, fly like a plane, etc.
Skate, skate, skate on the ice
Swim, swim, swim like a fish
Float, float, float like a leaf
Tip-toe-tip to my Lou
Walk, walk, walk to my Lou
Backwards, walk to my Lou
Sideways, walk to my Lou

Comments: The teacher needs firm yet gentle control when children are moving freely. There is a balance needed between freedom and structure. Too much freedom means children may bump each other and sabotage the game. Too much control may take the fun out of moving in one's own unique way. Experiment and see what works. You might start the game with just three or four children and add a few more with each verse.

Monkey See! Monkey Do!

Ages: 2¹/₂–6 years

Benefits: Body awareness (imitation of movement)
Balance and rhythmic coordination of body
Match of actions to their verbal labels

In Variation #1: Children practice opposites with language, actions, words.

Directions: Children can perform this game in a circle, but it is better if children scatter
so they have room to hop and jump. Children may learn the song by having
the teacher sing a line with actions, then children sing the line with actions.
See music with directions below.

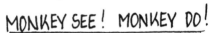

Repeat with spins, jumps, runs, kicks, shakes, wiggles, etc., whatever children choose.

Variation #1: Children practice singing and doing opposites.

Examples:

> The monkey talks real loud, LIKE THIS!
> The monkey talks real soft, like this [whisper].
> Monkey see, monkey do! The monkey talks the same as you.

> The monkey jumps real high like this [big jump]
> The monkey jumps real low like this [tiny jump]
> Monkey see, monkey do! The monkey jumps the same as you.

> The monkey stomps his foot like this [stomp hard]
> The monkey stomps his foot like this [stomp softly]
> Monkey see, monkey do! The monkey stomps the same as you.

Variation #2: Each child takes a turn being the leader.

Comments: This is a good rainy-day song, because it can provide a good workout (depending on the actions selected) in a short time, and provide a means for untensing those large muscles.

"This Old Man" Variations

(Active Musical Game)

Ages: 3–5 years

Directions: Children sing and act out whatever (gross motor) motion is being sung. They will act out these rhythmic movements while labeling them verbally. This game also helps develop body awareness.

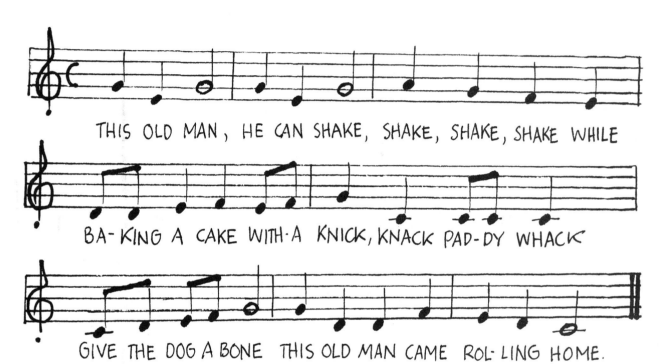

Verse 2:

This old man, he can jump,
Jump, jump, jump on a great big stump.
Knick-knack, paddy whack, give a dog a bone.
This old man came rolling home.

Verse 3:

This old man, he can skip,
Skip, skip, skip, be careful, don't trip.
Knick-knack, paddy whack, give a dog a bone.
This old man came rolling home.

Verse 4:

This old man, he can slide,
Slide, slide, slide while trying to hide.
Knick-knack, paddy whack, give a dog a bone.
This old man came rolling home.

Verse 5:

This old man, he can run,
Run, run, run and have some fun.
Knick-knack, paddy whack, give a dog a bone.
This old man came rolling home.

Verse 6:

This old man, he can sway,
Sway, sway, sway, and sway all day.
Knick-knack, paddy whack, give a dog a bone.
This old man came rolling home.

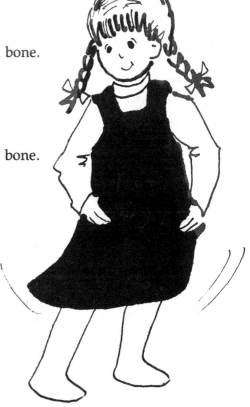

Mama Don't Allow

Ages: 3–6 years

American Folk Song

MA-MA DON'T 'LOW NO JUMP-IN' IN HERE

MA-MA DON'T 'LOW NO JUMP-IN' IN HERE

I DON'T CARE WHAT MA-MA DON'T 'LOW, I'M GON-NA JUMP

AN-Y HOW MA-MA DON'T 'LOW NO JUMP-IN' IN HERE.

"WE DON'T CARE"...

Directions: Children sing the first two lines standing still. When they reach the third line, "I don't care, etc.," they start the physical action—jumping, hopping, etc. Repeat the verse with other actions, alternating strenuous and quieter motions, and perhaps ending with "resting."

Other actions that children enjoy:

hopping

crawling

skipping

running

twisting

spinning

wiggling

sleeping

Variation:

You may want to allow children to start the physical motions at an earlier point in the song.

Comments: Little children think it's really funny to go against Mama's rules. No, you don't have to worry about reinforcing incorrect grammar. This little game helps young children develop a variety of gross motor skills, especially balance and coordination.

Ring Around the Rosey

(A New Movement Game)

Ages: 3–8 years

Benefits: Gross motor skills

Group cooperation and participation

Falling on cue

Coordination skills

Directions: Small groups: Skip, walk, or run freely around the room and *stoop down and touch the floor with finger tips* at the end of the song: "all fall down."

Large groups or limited space: *Walk* freely around the room and stoop down and touch the floor with finger tips at the end of the song.

Song:

Ring around the rosey

A pocketful of posies

Ashes, ashes

We all fall down.

Variations:

1. Skip or walk in the shape of the number 8, while singing.
2. Skip or walk with a partner while singing (hold your partner's hand and both go down at the same time; this will take a little more coordination than doing it by yourself).
3. Skip or walk with a partner while singing, but start walking and singing slowly, and gradually get faster in the moving and singing until you are running by the end of the song. Hold your partner's hand while doing this; it will take even more coordination!
4. Have groups of four holding hands and walking in a circle, dropping hands and touching the floor at the end of the song.

    Keep adding to the number in the groups. This will get harder for the students as the group gets larger—a good lesson in *group cooperation!*

Comments: On *all* of the variations, stoop down and touch the floor with finger tips at the end of the song. Do not actually fall down (less of a chance of getting hurt).

"Ten Little Indians"

(Variations)

Ages: 3, 4, and 5, with variations for each age

Verse 1 (age 3): Children march in single file around a large circle. The teacher keeps time with a drum or tom-tom.

> Lift one foot and then the other.
> Lift one foot and then the other.
> Lift one foot and then the other.
> Ten little Indian girls and boys.

Verse 2 (ages 3 & 4): Children hop in place.

> Hop on one foot, then the other.
> Hop on one foot, then the other.
> Hop on one foot, then the other.
> Ten little Indian girls and boys.

Verse 3 (ages 4 & 5): Children walk and hop around the circle.

> Walk and hop, and walk and hop now.
> Walk and hop, and walk and hop now.
> Walk and hop, and walk and hop now.
> Ten little Indian girls and boys.

Verse 4 (ages 5 & 6): Children hop four times on one foot, then four times on the other. Hop in place in slow motion without forward movement until the movement becomes easy. The teacher may call out "one-two-three-change" while the children are learning. Later add the music and verse:

> Hop four times and then the other.
> Hop four times and then the other.
> Hop four times and then the other.
> Ten little Indian girls and boys.

Comments: Expect a great deal of imperfection. It is quite a task to learn to hop to music, and for some children, they may never quite get the hang of changing feet at the proper time. The activity can still promote coordination, strength, balance, and fun.

Mouse Trap

(A Variation of "London Bridge")

Ages: 3½–6 years

Benefits: Alertness
Cooperative play

Equipment: A long rope or piece of twine to mark the circle.

Directions: Everyone has a role in this game. Each child is either a Mouse or a Trap. If possible, see that every child has a turn in each role. There are several ways to do this (see variations).

If your group is large, let six children form three Traps. They stand in pairs on the circle line, hands joining overhead to make three bridges. The other children, the Mice, walk underneath, around the circle.

Everyone sings, over and over, the "Mouse Verse" to the tune of "London Bridge."

At a special signal from the teacher (a drum thump), somewhere in the *middle* of the song, the Traps quickly but gently lower their arms, sometimes catching a Mouse. Any Mice caught in one of the traps become Traps, each joining another newly caught Mouse to make a new Trap.

CAUGHT IN A MOUSETRAP

MOUSE VERSE

LIT-TLE MICE ARE WALK-ING ROUND, WALK-ING ROUND, WALK-ING ROUND

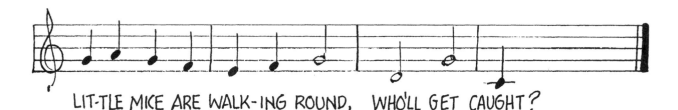

LIT-TLE MICE ARE WALK-ING ROUND, WHO'LL GET CAUGHT?

Variations and suggestions:

1. You can play the game without singing. Or you can use any of the original "London Bridge" verses. You can make up some additional verses about mice, such as "Little mice are caught inside," or "Little Mouse becomes a trap, etc."

2. If time is short, half the children could start out being Traps, and half could be Mice. After all Mice are caught, let those who started out as Traps be the Mice and vice versa.

3. Be sure to let Mice have several trips around the circle before starting the trapping process—so all Mice will feel they have had a good long turn.

4. Remind the Traps they may not lower the bridge until they hear the teacher's signal. **When the bridge (Trap) is lowered, it must be quickly but gently done. We don't want any Mice bumped on the head.**

5. Remind the Mice that they are not allowed to run, nor duck down to a kneeling position in order to escape getting caught.

Comments: Every child who tries this game falls in love with it. It is good for teaching gentleness and alertness. It also shows children that game rules can be fair and fun. You may want to explain that everyone gets caught, it's fun to get caught, and no one ever is eliminated from the game.

Dodge Ball

(Four Versions)

Ages: 5–11 years

Benefits: Social give and take
Alertness
Quick reactions in rolling, throwing, and dodging

Equipment: Large rubber playground ball
A large circle that is drawn, taped, or roped off on the floor or playground

Directions: If the group is small (say five to seven children), have one child stand in the center of a circle, the others stand around the circumference. The circle children roll the ball at the *feet* of the center child who attempts to dodge. When the center child is hit, she or he trades places with the successful roller. Make sure everyone gets a turn, perhaps by a "move up" number system.

If the group is larger (say ten or more), half the children may go into the center, the other half stand on the circumference. The ball is rolled back and forth. As each child is hit, he/she leaves the circle. After all the children are hit, or after a designated number of minutes, the teams change places.

If children tend to be hit before they have a chance to dodge, make the circle larger, or you may give young children a handicap, perhaps two hits before having to leave.

Variations:

A soft ball may be *thrown* at the child or children in the center, hitting them anywhere on the legs (or below the waist).

Or, have children stand around the circle, with one child in the center holding the ball. Each child (or each two children) are given a number or the same color. At a signal from the teacher ("Number threes run across"), the center child tries to roll (or throw) the ball at the running threes. If one is tagged, she/he changes places with the center child.

Comments: Make up whatever rules may be needed to give each child chances to be both runner and dodger.

Four Square

Ages: 6–12 years

Equipment: A rubber ball about 8 inches in diameter
Paint or chalk to draw a large square

Benefits: Eye-hand coordination
Aim, alertness and quick response
Social skills: taking turns, cooperation, problem solving
Balance

Directions: A large square is painted or drawn with chalk on concrete or blacktop. The sides of the square should be about 11 to 15 feet. The large square is divided into equal fourths, and the four small squares are numbered 1, 2, 3, 4.

Four children stand, one in each square. The child in square 1 serves from just outside the outside corner of square 1. He/she must serve underhand; the ball bounces into any of the other three squares and the receiving child must then direct the ball to any other square, where it should bounce once and again be hit underhand by another player.

The ball must not touch a line, nor may a player step on a line. The ball may not touch a player except on the hands, and must always be hit underhand.

If a player faults, he/she must yield the position. Everyone moves up. A new player is added, and the child leaving goes to the end of the waiting line (if any).

Hopscotch

Ages: 5 years and up

Benefits: Coordination of eyes and hands
Jumping skills
Following rules

Equipment: Chalk
Flat stone marker

Directions: The court can be drawn on concrete or blacktop in any of a variety of styles. The most simple is illustrated here:

One to four children can play at one time.

The first child throws his or her stone into square 1. The child hops over square 1 into squares 2 and 3 and on up the court, turns around in squares 8 & 9 and returns back down the court stopping to pick up the stone in square 1, hops into square 1, and out to the starting place.

If the child throws the stone into the given square without touching any lines and if the child successfully hops through the court without touching down with both feet (except for squares 2 & 3, 5 & 6, 8 & 9) and if the child successfully picks up the marker, then his or her turn continues until he or she misses.

Comments: This old favorite game can go on for hours of sociable fun.

Indian Ball

Ages: 6–12 years

Equipment: Softball and bat

A large play area, such as a large field

Directions: The batter stands at one end of the field. All other players are fielders and are scattered throughout the area. There can be any number of fielders. The object of the game is to catch the batted ball and thereby trade places with the batter.

The batter tosses the ball into the air and attempts to hit it into the field. (He is allowed to keep trying until he hits the ball.)

A fielder may become the batter in two ways:

1. If a fielder catches the ball on the fly, he or she becomes the batter.

2. If a fielder catches the ball on a ground roll, without fumbling, she then has a chance to become batter: She first must roll the ball and hit the bat, which has been placed on the ground in the batter's box.

   But, if the ball hits the bat and pops up, and if the batter then catches the ball on the fly, the batter gets to stay at bat.

Man from Mars

Ages: 5 years and up

Directions: One person is chosen to be "the Man from Mars." He/she stands in the middle of a playing field and all the other children gather together behind an agreed-upon boundary on one end of the playground or field. This boundary could be a fence, a line drawn on the field, a length of rope or twine, or portable markers. At this point the Man/Woman from Mars says:

> I'm the Man from Mars,
> I'll chase you to the stars
> If you have on
> [name a color, an object,
>   a certain birthday
>   month, or names that
>   begin with A, B, C,
>   etc.]

If the Man from Mars says, "If you have on red," all the children with red on must run out on the field or playground. The Man from Mars chases them. If anyone is tagged before he/she reaches the other end of the field (again marked for boundaries), he/she must join the Man from Mars in the middle of the field and assist him/her in tagging future children who are called out. Continue until all have been tagged. Then start over with a new Man or Woman from Mars.

Peanut Butter

Ages: 2–4 years. Older children can graduate to other forms of tag.

Benefits: Very good running exercise
Alertness

Directions: Establish two boundary lines indoors or out, far enough apart that children can break into a hard run. Children and teacher line up on one of the boundaries. The teacher then calls out the names of various foods, "oranges," "soup," "sandwiches," "milk." When the teacher calls "peanut butter," that is the signal for the children to run across to the other line, and for the teacher to chase them. Anyone caught pays no penalty and becomes a runner again. The teacher should do mostly chasing and little catching. The object of the game is to get healthful exercise, learn to listen for a signal, and of course, have fun. There should be no winners or losers. This is not a race.

Comments: Little children love this game. It is ridiculously simple, but a delight for them, good for fitness, and a healthy way to blow off steam.
Outdoors, play the game in a grassy area if possible.

Red Rover

Ages: 3–8 years

Benefits & Comments: This is a rousing and noisy game that children love. It provides vigorous exercise and, once learned, children can play it at school or in their home neighborhoods without adult supervision.

The game is well-suited to small groups. It helps develop social skills; also children learn to muster all their strength and speed to break through an "obstacle."

The game helps children go all out in an uninhibited game that is safe and intriguing. It's a way for shy children to learn to be forceful and to learn give and take.

Directions: Children line up as two teams facing each other across a running space of 15 or 20 feet. The teams alternate between being runners or receivers, for example:

The receiving team joins hands and calls to the runners, "Red Rover, Red Rover, let Patty (or whoever) come over." Patty runs across the field and tries to break through the chain of joined hands of the receiving team. If Patty succeeds in breaking through the line, she may pick one child from that team (the receivers) to return with her to her own team. If she doesn't break through, she joins the receiving team.

Now the other team takes a turn to call over someone from the other side. There are elements of strategy involved as runners decide where in the receiving line they will "attack," and receivers learn how to strengthen weak places in their line.

Rules may be varied by the teacher to suit the needs of the group. For example, one team may get a lot larger right away, in which case some children may volunteer to go over to the other side.

Usually children decide whom to call over, but the teacher may make suggestions if some children need a turn to run.

Pre-Relay and Easy Relay Races

Ages: For Pre-Relays: Kindergarten and first grade

For Relays: second grade and up

Benefits: Provides: tension release

Experience following simple rules

Social skills

Equipment: A couple of beanbags for the pre-relays

For many relays, no equipment is needed.

Comments: Races involve team competition, which may be hard on young children. For this reason, relay races should be very easy; are best engaged in by children of grade 2 and up. Winning and losing can be downplayed. Teams should be chosen by the teacher, not by team captains, since this is hurtful to those last chosen. Teams should be balanced for age and ability as much as possible. Several small teams (three or four members) ensure less waiting and more participation. Less skilled children should be placed in the middle, not in first or last position.

Pre-relays:

(For kindergartners and first graders). *Circle Relay*: Children in each of two small circles pass a beanbag around the circle. The first team returning the beanbag to its starting place wins a point. Gradually add two trips around the circle, etc.

Side-by-Side Relay: Children stand side-by-side in two lines. Each team passes a beanbag down the line on the word "go." The team that completes the task first wins a point.

Variation: The beginnings of team member rotation can be introduced by having the last person in line run with the beanbag up to the head of the line. Gradually add the concept of *each* end-of-the-line member carrying the beanbag to the starting place at the head of the line.

Easy Relays:

Children may do some simple task at the turn-around point, such as:

- Touch a base, wall or pole and return to their starting line
- Bounce a ball once at the turn-around point
- Jump twice at the turn-around point

Children may do some simple task on the way up and back, such as:

- Jumping with feet together
- Bouncing a ball (dribbling)
- Running forward and walking backward to the starting place

Variations of Tag

(Wood Tag, Shadow Tag, Stoop Tag)

Ages: 5–10 years

Benefits: Running, dodging, quick-thinking skills. Healthful exercise, gives children who've been cooped up a chance to stretch and blow off steam.

Directions: For kindergartners, the teacher should be "It" for the first few run-throughs. Then a new "It" can be chosen.

Whoever is "It" covers his/her eyes and counts slowly to five. The rest of the children scatter, being sure to stay within pre-arranged boundaries. (A smaller field for young children, larger for older ones.) "It" tries to tag (gently) one of the running children who becomes the new "It."

Wood Tag:

Children are safe if they are touching wood: a tree, a wood fence, a building, a stick, a toy.

Shadow Tag:

Children are safe in the shade or shadows.

Stoop Tag:

Children are safe when they are in a stooped position.

Comments: Teachers must use their imaginations in order to ensure that everyone gets a turn to be "It," over a period of two days. Make up a temporary rule, such as: children who haven't been "It" yet must stay within an area closer to where "It" starts to run.

If you have a child who can't run well at all (say a partially disabled child), you can help him or her to get into the fun by reducing the boundaries, so that the other children have a harder time escaping. Keep "pulling in" the boundaries until someone gets caught, or give the runner a three-minute time limit, after which he/she chooses the next "It."

You can use the game as an occasion to explain very simply that in golf and in many athletic competitions, a "handicap" may be given to equalize the odds for all players. Of course you do this in a way that will not put down any less-abled children that you may have.

It is assumed that in the extended-day classroom, there will be a variety of ages and a wide variety of levels of skill. You can make various adjustments so that younger and older children can play together. Giving a "handicap" is just one way of equalizing the challenge of the game. Other ways are: (1) to divide the class so that two groups can play separate games of tag, or (2) one group can be busy with another activity while the other group plays tag.

Any running game may result in falls, or some children may inadvertently be too rough when tagging. Plan your tag games for a grassy area if possible. And explain before the game starts, that we should tag gently, without grabbing or poking. A tag game can teach many give-and-take social skills as well as physical skills.

Telephone Game

(And New Variation)

Ages: 5 years and up

Benefits: Auditory skills
Group cooperation
Memory retention

Directions: Have everyone sit in a circle.

A message will be passed around the circle, from child to child, by whispering the message in a neighbor's ear. (Be careful not to whisper loud enough so anyone else can hear.) Example: "You are fantastic!"

When the message has gone around the whole circle, have the last child say the message out loud so everyone can hear. (It's always fun to hear how the message got mixed up along the way!)

Variation:

Choose five to ten children to leave the room.

Tell a very short story to the rest of the group and then call the children back into the room, one by one.

Tell the first child the story and then call another child into the room. The first child has to relay the story to the second child without any help from the rest of the group.

Call a third child into the room and the second child has to relay the story to the third child, again without any help from the rest of the group.

Keep calling the children back into the room until everyone has been called. Be sure to tell the rest of the group not to give away any of the story or try to correct the one saying the story. (This is where group cooperation comes in!)

Comments: Start off with a very short message or story so everyone can understand the game, then you can make the message or story longer and longer.

The longer the message or story, the funnier the end result will be.

Tell-a-Story

Ages: 5 years and up

Benefits: Language development
                 Quick thinking
                 Concentration

Directions: Children sit in a circle.

One child starts to tell a story. After two or three sentences, he or she stops and the next child has to continue the story, again only using two or three sentences.

Continue the story until everyone has had a turn.

This is not cumulative, you do not repeat what the previous child has said, only add to their story.

Variation:

Instead of going around the circle and having each child take a turn with the story, have the teacher point to different children and they have to continue the story.

If you do not take turns in order, the children have to pay attention more and think faster if they are called on.

Comments: It is easier for the smaller children if you tell them to tell a story about something they have already done, maybe describe a field trip they went on, or retell a well-known story.

Once the little ones get used to the idea of adding onto a story, they can then start to create their own.

Shopping Trip

Ages: 6 years and up

Benefits: Concentration

Memory retention

Directions: Have children sit in a circle.

Talk about going to the food store and have children name some of the foods you might find at the store.

After several minutes of talking about foods, start the game. (This is a cumulative activity so everyone has to pay attention to what is being said.)

Game:

Teacher: I went to the store and bought some <u>bananas</u>.

First child, on teacher's right: I went to the store and bought some <u>bananas</u> and <u>candy</u>.

Second child: I went to the store and bought some <u>bananas</u>, <u>candy</u>, and <u>hot dogs</u>.

Third child: I went to the store and bought some <u>bananas</u>, <u>candy</u>, <u>hot dogs</u>, and <u>ice cream</u>.

Keep going around the circle until everyone has had a turn.

Variation 1:

To make the game more difficult, use the letters of the alphabet. Foods must follow that order: <u>a</u>pples, <u>b</u>roccoli, <u>c</u>orn, <u>d</u>oughnuts, <u>e</u>ggs, <u>f</u>lour, etc.

Variation 2:

Only name foods from specific categories, such as fruits or vegetables.

Older children could learn the four major food groups: (1) meats, poultry, and fish; (2) cereals and grains; (3) milk and dairy products; (4) fruits and vegetables.

Comments: This is the type of game that children can play by themselves, in small groups, once they learn the rules.

My Name is Alice

Ages: 9 years and up

Benefits: Coordination
                Concentration
                Motor skills
                Group cooperation
                Language development

Equipment: Jump rope
                Ball for variations

Directions: Have children think of boys' and girls' names; and cities, states or countries that start with the same first letter as the name.

See if the children can go through the whole alphabet and pick a name and geographical site for each letter.

Have two children hold a long jump rope, one on each end of the rope, and start to swing the rope to a steady beat.

Other children will form a single line and, one by one, will take turns jumping inside the rope while saying:

> First child: [jump in and say while jumping:]
>   My name is <u>Alice</u> and I come from <u>Alabama</u> [jump out]
> Second child: [jump in and say while jumping:]
>   My name is <u>Barbara</u> and I come from the <u>Bahamas</u> [jump out]
> Third child: My name is <u>Carl</u> and I come from <u>Carolina</u> [jump out]
> Fourth child: My name is <u>David</u> and I come from <u>Denver</u> [jump out]

As you take your turn, go to the end of the line. Continue until you have gone through the whole alphabet.

Variation 1:

This can be done by one child only, with one jump rope. She (or he) can see how far along she can get in the alphabet without touching the rope and stopping the skipping. Each time she stops, she has to start from "A" again.

Variation 2:

Instead of a jump rope, one child could use a large or small ball and bounce the ball steadily while saying the names.

If you are using a small ball, make it more difficult by switching hands to bounce the ball after each name:

> Right hand: My name is Alice, etc.
> Left hand: My name is Barbara, etc.

3

SONGS
and
FINGERGAMES

Both speech and reading are rhythmic activities. Songs and fingergames are pleasant ways of utilizing language in a rhythmic manner.

Songs and fingergames are also useful and interesting ways of filling in transition times, including waiting for the bus, for snacks, or for parents. They help make a rainy day cheerful. They help build a feeling of group solidarity and contribute to a sense of humor.

See also pages 163 to 174 for directions for making simple musical instruments. Many of the songs and some fingergames include the use of instruments as a variation.

The benefits occurring to specific songs and fingergames have not been listed because they are universal to all these activities and include:

- *Language skills:* use of complete sentences, grammatical structure, additions to vocabulary.
- *Coordination of words and music:* In the case of fingergames, also coordination of actions, words, and often music. These build listening skills and concentration.
- *Social studies:* origins of ethnic or folk songs.
- *Social skills:* group cooperation and unity, playfulness, and humor.

Familiar Folk Songs

Folk songs are first sung, and then written down. No one person makes these tunes. They are the product of people gathering together to sing. The folk songs included here are just for that purpose—singing for the joy of singing. Some include interesting activities to accompany them.

Swing Low, Sweet Chariot

Variation: When children can sing both "Swing Low, Sweet Chariot" and "All Night, All Day," try singing them together. Remember that "Swing Low" starts on an upbeat, so that the words "low" and "All" will be sung together on Beat 1. The rhythm of "All Night" is twice as fast as "Swing Low," although both songs are sung quite slowly. You will also notice that the Chorus comes first in both songs, followed by the verse. Chorus is then repeated. When singing the songs together, omit the verses or sing them separately.

BARNYARD SONG

Kentucky Mountain Song

I HAD A CAT AND MY CAT PLEASED ME. I FED MY CAT UN-DER

YON-DER TREE. CAT GOES FID-DLE-I - EE. 2. I HAD A

HEN AND THE HEN PLEASED ME. I FED MY HEN UN-DER YON-DER TREE.

HEN GOES CHIM-MY CHUCK, CHIM-MY CHUCK, CAT GOES FID-DLE-I- EE.

I HAD A DUCK AND THE DUCK PLEASED ME. I FED MY DUCK UN-DER

YON-DER TREE. DUCK GOES QUACK, QUACK. HEN GOES CHIM-MY CHUCK,

CHIM-MY CHUCK. CAT GOES FID-DLE-I - EE

Verses:

4. Goose goes swishy, swashy
5. Sheep goes baa, baa
6. Hog goes griffy, gruffy
7. Cow goes moo, moo
8. Horse goes neigh, neigh

Repeat all previous animal sounds. This is a cumulative song.

Variation:

Children can be assigned to be the different animals. Each child sings his/her part as it occurs in the song and in the repetition.

Paper bag puppets might be fun to make, decorating each bag to be a different animal.

The Animal Fair

Variation:

When the group knows this song very well it is fun to add a second part. Everyone sings the song through to the end, and then a small group continues singing over and over again "the monk, the monk, the monk" (see example below). As soon as this chant is steady, the rest of the group sings the whole song over again.

Cuckoo

Austria

OH I WENT TO PE-TER'S FLOW-ING SPRING WHERE THE WA-TER'S SO

GOOD AND I HEARD THERE THE CUC-'KOO AS SHE CALLED FROM THE WOOD HO-LE-AH

CHORUS

HO-LE-RAH-HI-HI-OH, HO-LE-RAH CUC-KOO HO-LE-RAH HI-HI-AH, HO-LE-RAH CUC-KOO

HO-LE-RAH HI-HI-AH, HO-LE-RAH CUC-KOO, HO-LE-RAH HI-HI-AH — HO .

Motions for Chorus:

 = alternating hands, pat your knees very fast

1 = slap knees

2 = clap hands

3 = snap fingers

* = snap fingers once on 1st verse, twice on 2nd and three times on 3rd verse.

Verse 2:

After Easter come sunny days
That will melt all the snow
Then I'll marry my maiden fair
We'll be happy I know.

CHORUS

Verse 3:

When I've married my maiden fair
What then can I desire?
Oh a home for her tending
And some wood for the fire.

CHORUS

Riddle Song

Ages: 6–12

Verse 2:

> How can there be a cherry that has no stone?
> How can there be a chicken that has no bone?
> How can there be a ring that has no end?
> How can there be a baby with no cryin'?

Verse 3:

> A cherry when it's blooming, it has no stone.
> A chicken when it's pipping, it has no bone.
> A ring when it's rolling, it has no end.
> A baby when it's sleeping, there's no cryin'.

Variation:

Enjoy here all the first-grade riddles. Perhaps suggest that children take turns making up their own, or bringing in some of their favorites.

Riddles

Ages: 6 years and up (Younger children don't understand the play on words.)

Directions: Children can use their minds and be creative in making up their own riddles.

1. What has eyes and cannot see?
2. What has a tongue and cannot talk?
3. What has legs and cannot walk?
4. What has arms and can't hug me?
5. What has legs and cannot crawl?
6. What is black and white and read all over?
7. What has ears but cannot hear?
8. What has a head but no hair?
9. What has hands but cannot wash?
10. What has a mouth but cannot talk?
11. What has a body but cannot wiggle?
12. What is it that never asks questions but always is answered?
13. What gives milk and has one horn?
14. What goes up white and comes down yellow and white?
15. What has a shoulder but no arm?
16. What kind of a room has no doors, no windows, no walls?

Answers:

1. needle or potato	9. clock
2. shoes	10. cave
3. table	11. guitar
4. chair	12. telephone or doorbell
5. table or chair	13. milk truck
6. newspaper	14. an egg
7. corn	15. a road
8. lettuce	16. mushroom

Comments: Some of these riddles were originated by first graders.

Riddles provide an excellent means of language development. Children learn to enjoy word-play.

Little Wheel A-Turnin' in My Heart

THERE'S A LIT-TLE WHEEL A-TURN-IN' IN MY HEART. THERE'S A
LIT-TLE WHEEL A-TURN-IN' IN MY HEART. IN MY HEART —— IN MY
HEART — THERE'S A LIT-TLE WHEEL A-TURN-IN' IN MY HEART.

Verse 2: There's a little foot a-tapping in my heart.

Verse 3: There's a little finger clicking in my heart.

Verse 4: There are little hands a-clapping in my heart.

Motions to accompany each verse:

1. Roll hands around each other—occasionally reversing and going the other way.
2. Tap foot lightly to the beat.
3. Click fingers of both hands alternately.
4. Clap hands to the beat.

Comments: This is a song that lends itself to many variations. For example: add instruments (drum beating, bell ringing, etc.) or make up your own verses.

Zum Gali Gali

Zum Gali Gali is an Israeli song that can be divided into two parts. One part is the repetitive chant and the other is the various verses of the song. It is very easy to learn the verses since there are only six Hebrew words. "Zum Gali, Gali" is pronounced "Zoom, gah-lee, gah-lee." The song is praising the pioneer and hoping for peace.

Directions: Teach everyone the Zum Gali, Gali chant first. Next teach the first verse, pointing out that there are only three words and the second time they are reversed. This pattern is repeated throughout. Use the pronunciation guide to learn to say the words. When you are ready to put the two parts together, let the chanting persons sing through their pattern first, and then bring in the group singing the verses. Watch the entrance of the verse part—it comes immediately *after* group 1 sings, "Zum."

Verses:

2. A-vo-dah le'man he-cha-lutz;
   He-cha-lutz le'man a-vo-dah.

3. He-cha-lutz le'man ha-b'tulah;
   Ha-b'tulah le'man he-cha-lutz.

4. Ha-sha-lom le'man ha'a-min;
   Ha-'a-min le'man ha-sha-lom.

Pronunciation guide:

a as in *father;* he like *hay;* le very short *e;*
i as in *machine;* o as in *come;* u as in *rule;*
ch as in German *ach.*

Beetles and the Bedbugs

Ages: 4–9 years

Directions: Say the chant through once using a normal tone of voice. Repeat the chant but start at a whisper and gradually go to a shout:

Line 1:   whisper
Line 2:   soft voice
Line 3:   normal voice
Line 4:   shout

Repeat the chant but go from a shout to a whisper.
Say the chant crying, laughing, angry, etc.

Chant:

I woke up Sunday morning and looked upon the wall,
The beetles and the bedbugs were having a game of ball.
The score was two to nothing and the beetles were ahead,
Then the bedbugs hit a homer and they knocked me out of bed!

Variations:

1. Use as a jump rope activity and jump rope while saying the rhyme but jump away from the rope on the word, "knocked" (this needs to be done with two other people holding the rope while one child jumps).

2. Also, imitate jumping a rope with an imaginary rope (each child will have his or her imaginary rope) and then jump to the side on the word, "knocked."

3. Add second verse:

I went down to my breakfast,
The bread was hard and stale,
The coffee tasted like tobacco juice,
Right out of the county jail!

4. Instead of chanting, sing with the following melody:

BEETLES AND THE BEDBUGS

I WOKE UP SUN-DAY MORN-ING AND LOOKED UP-ON THE WALL, THE

BEE-TLES AND THE BED-BUGS WERE HAV-ING A GAME OF BALL. THE

SCORE WAS TWO TO NOTH-ING AND THE BEE-TLES WERE A-HEAD, THEN THE

BED-BUGS HIT A HOM-ER AND THEY KNOCKED ME OUT OF BED!

The Consonant Song

(A Hilarious Tongue Twister)

Ages: 5–12 years

Directions: Have children name the vowels: write them on the board. Perhaps sing the conventional "Alphabet Song" (A, B, C, D, E, F, G, etc.).

Explain that in this new song, we use the consonants. Write some or all on the board.

We will take each consonant and fit it into a silly little rhyme. Each verse is identical to all other verses *except* for the consonant used.

Ask children, what's the first letter in the alphabet? "A" is the answer, but we can't use "A" because it's a vowel. So we start with "B." Here is the verse. Practice it slowly at first, but with a definite rhythm. (Actually, we're adding "B" to various long vowels.)

B- A - BAY, B- E- BEE B- I - BIT-TY-BYE, B-ō - BO BIT-TY

BYE- BŌ - BĒ -BOO - BOO BIT-TY BYE BŌ   BOO-BOO!

Now try adding other consonants in place of the "B." For example, "D":

D - A - DAY
D - E - DEE
D - I - DITTY-DYE
D - O   DOUGH

DITTY DYE, DOUGH, DEE, DOO
DOO, DITTY DYE, DOUGH, DOO-DOO!

Comments: It's easy once you get onto it—hard the first time or two. This funny chant is guaranteed to banish the doldrums on a long rainy day.

The Doughnut Shoppe

Ages: 3–8 years

Materials: None, though children around 5 or 6 may enjoy a jump rope (six feet long).

Directions: Children may clap to the chant; jump to it or jump rope to it. Younger ones may treat the chant as a fingerplay. Older children may do a pease-porridge-hot, simple or complex clapping pattern.

The chant:

I walked around the corner, [walk with fingers]
And I walked around the block
And I walked right up [swing arms]
To the doughnut shoppe. [open door]
I grabbed me a doughnut [grabbing motion]
And I licked off the grease, [licking motion]
And I handed the lady [hand-over motion]
A five-cent piece.
Well, she looked at the nickel [looks at palm]
And she looked at me.
And she said, "This nickel's [shake head]
    no good for me."
"There's a hole in the nickel,
    [hold hand up, look through]
    I can see right through."
"Well, lady, there's a hole
    [form hole with fingers]
    in the doughnut, too."

————

Thanks for the doughnut, You bet.

THANKS FOR THE DOUGH-NUT, YOU BET

Hand Jive Routines

Ages: 7 years and up

"Hand Jive" can be used to accompany any music, but it is particularly effective with Rock 'n' Roll pieces. The idea is to plan a few routines with your hands that are then repeated over and over again as the music is played. Of course, the routines follow the beat of this infectious music.

In the beginning you might start with just four routines; after some practice, try all eight. Keep repeating these patterns until the song ends.

	Beat 1	**Beat 2**	**Beat 3**	**Beat 4**
1.	Click fingers	Click fingers	Click fingers	Click fingers
2.	Tap left fist with right fist	Tap right fist with left fist	repeat	repeat
3.	Bend right arm tap elbow twice	Bend left arm tap elbow twice	repeat	repeat

	Beat 1	Beat 2	Beat 3	Beat 4
4.	Cool wave right	Cool wave left	repeat	repeat
5.	Palms down, cross hands in front of you—two beats for each crossover, right hand on top first	repeat	repeat	repeat
6.	Hitchhike over right shoulder	Hitchhike over left shoulder	repeat	repeat
7.	Zigzag your hands over your head alternately	repeat	repeat	repeat

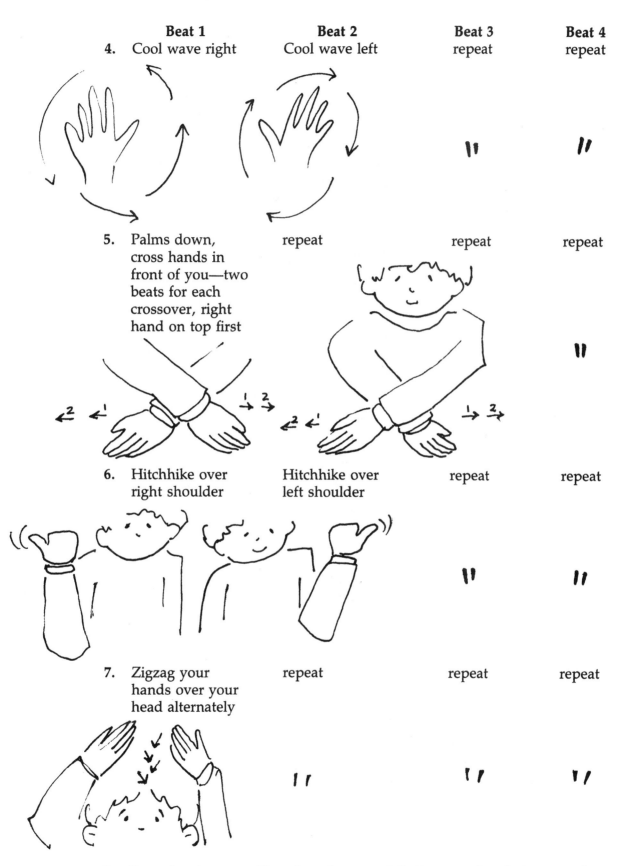

8. Spread out arms with palms down and flutter your hands in toward your body for four beats.

Head and Shoulders, Baby

Ages: 6–8 years (some 5-year-olds can do a simple version)

Directions & Verse: The game consists of quickly touching two designated body parts, with simple (or with older children, complex pat-a-cake or pease-porridge-hot) clapping patterns. Teach a simple pattern, then later encourage children to improvise their own original clapping patterns, with or without a partner.

Verse 1:

Head and shoulders, baby, one, two, three
Head and shoulders, baby, one, two, three
Head and shoulders, head and shoulders
Head and shoulders, baby, one, two, three.

Verse 2:

Shoulders—waist, baby, one, two, three
Shoulders—waist, baby, one, two, three
Shoulders—waist, shoulders and waist
Shoulders—waist, baby, one, two, three.

Verse 3:

Waist and hips, baby, one, two, three
Waist and hips, baby, one, two, three
Waist and hips, waist and hips
Waist and hips baby, one, two, three.

Verse 4:

Hips and knees, baby, one, two, three
Hips and knees, baby, one, two, three
Hips and knees, hips and knees
Hips and knees, baby, one, two, three.

Verse 5:

Knees and toes, baby, one, two, three
Knees and toes, baby, one, two, three
Knees and toes, knees and toes
Knees and toes, baby, one, two, three.

Verse 6:

That's all baby (turn around) one, two, three
That's all baby, one, two, three
That's all baby, that's all baby
That's all baby, one, two, three.

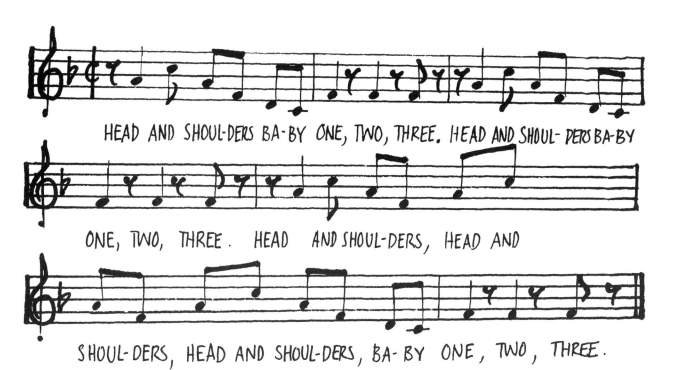

HEAD AND SHOUL-DERS BA-BY ONE, TWO, THREE. HEAD AND SHOUL-DERS BA-BY

ONE, TWO, THREE.   HEAD   AND SHOUL-DERS,   HEAD AND

SHOUL-DERS, HEAD AND SHOUL-DERS, BA-BY ONE, TWO, THREE.

Miss Sue

(Another Version)

Ages: 4–8 years

Directions: This is a funny fingergame that children often do while standing up. It is a favorite playground or street game that children play over and over among themselves.

> Miss Sue, Miss Sue,
> Miss Sue from Alabama.
> Little Baby Walker [hands under chin]
> Sitting in a rocker [rock body, knees bent]
> Eating Betty Crocker [stir and eat, while rocking]
> A, B, C, D, E, F, G, [alternately pat hands to chest and stomach]
> H, I, J, K, L, M, N, O, P,
> Q, R, S, T, U, and V,
> W, X, and Y and Z.
> Wash that spot right off of me [rub hands together]
>
> Moochi-con, ["spray" fingers out, like sprinkling water]
> Moochi-con,
> Moochi-con,
> Freeze! [forefinger points]
>
> Moochi-con, ["spray" fingers out]
> Moochi-con,
> Moochi-con,
> Freeze! [forefinger points]

"MOOCHI-CON"

Under the Spreading Chestnut Tree

(Chant)

Ages: 3–6 years

Directions: Children sit or stand, in a circle, so they can see and enjoy each other's actions.

They say the verse and perform the motions together.

Chant:

Under the spreading   chest - nut   tree

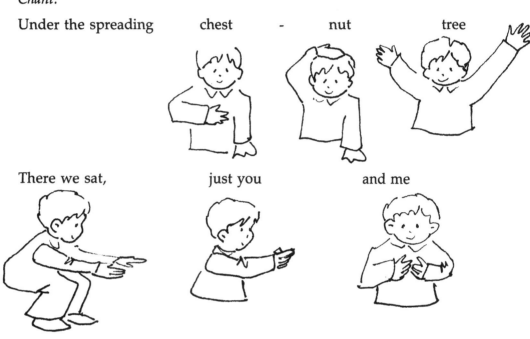

There we sat,   just you   and me

Oh how happy we would be

Under the spreading   chest - nut   tree

Comments: This chant may be an old chestnut to adults but it will be new to children. They enjoy its broad, obvious humor.

When I Was a Little Girl (Boy)

Ages: 4–6 years

WHEN I WAS A LIT-TLE GIRL, LIT-TLE GIRL, LIT-TLE GIRL

WHEN I WAS A LIT-TLE GIRL (5, 4, 3) YEARS OLD.   I

ROCKED MY DOL-LY THIS-A-WAY, THAT-A-WAY, THIS-A-WAY. I

ROCKED MY DOL-LY THIS-A-WAY   ALL   DAY   LONG.

Other activities very young children do:

rolled a ball	jumped around
shook my rattle	hugged my daddy (mommy)
held my bottle	petted Fido
ran around	crept and crawled

Variations: Instead of "all day long," sing "one year old," "two years old," etc. You could work up to activities children do at the age they are now.

Instead of "little girl" or "little boy," you might prefer to use "little child" or "little kid."

Comments: Children think of the activities they used to do and/or still do. The song reminds them that they're bigger now and they can do more things. The song encourages affection for the child they once were and pride in growing up.

The teacher might want to avoid using only stereotypical girls' activities or boys' activities. For example, boys could "rock a dolly" and girls could "roll a ball." It might be fun to reverse the stereotypes deliberately and explain to the children why you're doing this.

The Witch Song

Ages: 3–8 years

Materials: Simple rhythm instruments, or sound-makers readily available, such as: pencils, paper to rattle, etc., can be added as a variation.

Directions: Learn the song as written and then let the children take turns making up their own witch's tune. Additional verses and accompanying spooky sounds can also be created by the children. Try to make the second and fourth phrases rhyme.

I AM AN OLD, OLD WITCH. I RIDE UP-ON MY BROOM. I

FRIGH-TEN ALL THE BOYS AND GIRLS WHEN I SING MY LONE-SOME TUNE.

OO - - - OO - - OO - - OO - - OO - - OO - - OO - - OO - - OO - - OO .

Additional verses:

I am a skinny old skeleton
I run and rattle my bones,
I frighten all the girls and boys,
When I peek into their homes.
    [followed by tongue-clicking, finger snapping, etc.]

I am a scary old ghost,
I float across the moon,
I frighten all the girls and boys,
When they're sleeping in their rooms.
    [followed by voices which slide from high to low and vice versa and
    range from soft to loud all on the syllable "oo."]

I am an old vampire,
I like to eat your skin,
I frighten all the girls and boys,
When I try to bite a chin.
    [strange sounds of laughter]

I am a squeaky bat,
I fly all through the air,
I frighten all the girls and boys,
When I try to grab their hair.
    [ask the children to come up with sounds for this one!]

Variations:

Rhythm instruments and other sound-makers can be substituted for the vocal and body sounds.

Comments: This is a dramatic song to act out with costumes on Halloween. All of the verses were written by the 5-year-old children at Wilson School. You can make it special for your children by having them write their own verses.

Familiar Rounds

Rounds are short songs (usually not more than three or four phrases) that are easily learned and fun to sing. When children know the round well, they can break into two or three groups and have each group start the round at a different time. All agree ahead of time on how many times they will sing the round through. Of course, if each group starts at a different time, they will end at a different time giving one the sense that the music goes "round and round."

The music is marked into sections 1, 2, 3, etc. so that you know how to start the different groups. Example: when group one reaches section 2 of the round, group two begins singing section 1 simultaneously, and so on.

CHAIRS TO MEND

Comment: This round dates back to street vendors and the calls they made as they went through the streets.

KOOKABURRA

Australian Round

KOO-KA-BUR-RA SITS ON AN OLD GUM TREE, MER-RY, MER-RY KING OF THE

BUSH IS HE, LAUGH KOO-KA BUR-RA, LAUGH KOO-KA BUR-RA, GAY YOUR LIFE MUST BE.

Comments: The Kookaburra is an Australian bird about the size of a crow whose call resembles loud laughter. This is a four-part round, but it is suggested that much practice be done with just two parts before you attempt to do four.

WHIPPOORWILL

GONE TO BED IS THE SET-TING SUN, NIGHT IS COM-ING AND

DAY IS DONE, WHIP-POOR WILL, WHIP-POOR-WILL, HAS JUST BE-GUN.

Comments: This is not a city bird, but you will never forget its call once you hear it on a quiet evening at twilight. Both of these songs would be fun to learn when you are making bird feeders. You can sing them as you work.

Lovely Evening

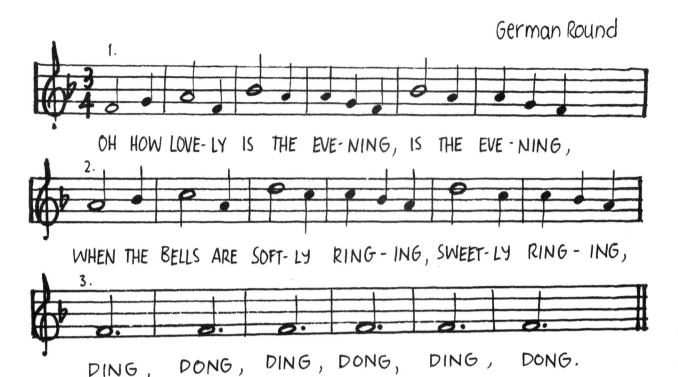

German Round

OH HOW LOVE-LY IS THE EVE-NING, IS THE EVE-NING,

WHEN THE BELLS ARE SOFT-LY RING-ING, SWEET-LY RING-ING,

DING,   DONG,   DING,   DONG,   DING,   DONG.

Comments: Easy to sing. In slow waltz time. *Long sustained* pealing of the bells in the last phrase.

On a cold, wintry day you might like to try a movement activity with this round. Teach it to everybody at one time and practice until they know it thoroughly. Then divide the group into three circles and start each of the circles' movements as you start the round. Just as you will hear three different phrases at once, so will you see three different movements at once.

Directions: *Phrase 1*

Starting on the right foot, walk counterclockwise on the circle, moving a foot only on the first and third beats and alternating feet.

Phrase 2

Reverse and move clockwise on the circle, only on the first and third beats.

Phrase 3

Face the center of the circle and sway gently back and forth changing feet on every third beat (on "ding" "dong").

Shalom Chaverim

Israeli Round

SHA-LOM CHA-VE-RIM, SHA-LOM CHA-VE-RIM, SHA-LOM, SHA-LOM. LE
HIT-RA-OT, LE HIT-RA-OT, SHA-LOM, SHA-LOM.

*All other groups enter at this spot. It is best to practice with just two parts.

Comments: This is a very good song to end a day whether it is sung as a round or not. "Shalom" is a Hebrew greeting used in many ways. It means, "peace."

MAKE NEW FRIENDS

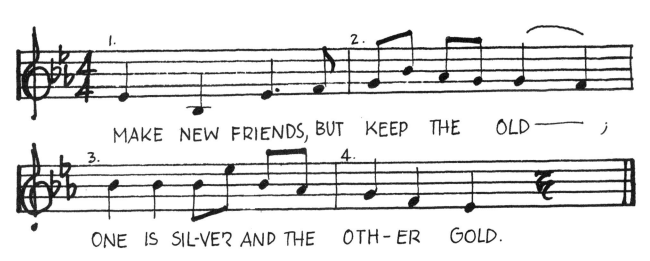

MAKE NEW FRIENDS, BUT KEEP THE OLD——;
ONE IS SIL-VER AND THE OTH-ER GOLD.

Comments: Another four-part round which should be sung many times in two parts before attempting four. Try humming it in a round instead of singing.

Apples

Rita Shotwell

Ages: 4–8 years

Directions: Chant the words and use the hand jive below each line. (Go over the hand jive first before practicing the words.)

Apples, apples on a tree,
[Four punches in mid air with right hand.]

Sweet as sweet as they can be,
[Four punches in mid air with left hand.]

Reach up high and grab me some,
[Roll arms one over the other four times.]

We'll make a pie and have some fun!
[Reach up with right hand, touch palm of left hand with right fingers, brush right hand up from left hand, stamp one foot.]

Slice those apples nice and thick,
[Four punches in mid air with right hand.]

Hurry, hurry make it quick,
[Four punches in mid air with left hand.]

Sugar, cinnamon, and butter too,
[Roll arms one over the other four times.]

Mix them up and that will do.
[Reach up with right hand, touch palm of left hand with right fingers, brush right hand up from left hand, stamp one foot.]

Roll that dough nice and thin,
[Four punches with right hand.]

Then we'll put some apples in,
[Four punches with left hand.]

Bake that pie nice and slow
[Roll arms one over the other four times.]

Then we'll eat, get ready, GO!!
[Reach up with right hand, touch palm of left hand with right fingers, brush right hand up from left hand, stamp one foot.]

Comments: Can also be sung to the tune of "Ham Bone."

I Am Special

Rita Shotwell

Ages: 4–6 years

Directions: Children sit in a circle. The teacher says the chant through once, inserting the color of his/her eyes and hair and then ends the chant with a big smile. Tell the class they have to smile back.

Each person will say the chant through once, inserting the color of his/her eyes and hair and ending with a big smile. Keep reminding the class that everyone must return the smile.

Chant:

Hey, hey look at me.
[Wave two times, once on each "hey,"
point to your self twice on "look at me."]

I am special, can't you see?
[Tuck thumbs under arm pits and
push chest forward in a "proud-like" gesture.]

My eyes are _____
[Point to your eyes and name their color.]

My hair is _____
[Point to hair and name the color.]

And I have a big smile to pass around.
[Give the class a big smile.]

Comments: If you are working with a small group of children, it's fun to pass the smile around the circle each time the chant is said. The person who says the chant will start the smile going around the circle. Children enjoy watching the smiling faces turn as the smile is passed around the circle. Sooner or later, some children will make funny faces as they pass their smiles on. That gets the group laughing and the smiles become very genuine.

This little game encourages social give and take, and puts everyone in a good mood.

Mac, Mac

Rita Shotwell

Ages: 3–7 years

Materials: Rhythm instruments for variation

Directions: Say the chant and have children do the actions with you. Can be done seated or standing.

Chant:

Mac, Mac his lips go smack [smack lips four times]
Rose, Rose, she wiggles her nose [wiggle nose four times]
Cy, Cy, he winks his eye [wink four times]
Dear, Dear, now pull your ear [pull ear four times]
Ned, Ned, he nods his head [nod head four times]

Variation #1:

Divide class into five small groups. Each group will play one type of rhythm instrument on one line only of the chant, while the teacher says the words. For example:

Line 1 (Mac): This group will play tone blocks with mallets.

Line 2 (Rose): This group will play maracas.

Line 3 (Cy): This group will play triangles.

Line 4: (Dear): This group will play bells.

Line 5 (Ned): This group will play rhythm sticks.

Variation #2:

Divide class into five small groups and each group will do actions:

Line 1 (Mac): This group will smack lips, continuing to the end of the chant.

Line 2 (Rose): This group will wiggle their noses and continue to end.

Line 3 (Cy): This group will wink one eye and continue to end.

Line 4 (Dear): This group will pull one ear and continue to end.

Line 5 (Ned): This group will nod their heads and continue to end.

My Face

Rita Shotwell

Ages: 5–10 years

Directions: Say the chant with the actions several times so everyone will be at ease with the actions.

Say the chant four times, each time eliminating an italicized word and doing the action for that word instead. So that everyone will start off the same, say: "One, two, ready, go," then touch your chest and eliminate the word, "my". Do this *each time* you come to the word "My."

The second time you say the chant, eliminate the word "face" and touch your face. You will now have two words that you eliminated and are doing actions only.

The third time you say the chant, eliminate the word "two" and hold up two fingers. Now you have three words that you eliminated and are doing only actions.

The fourth time you say the chant, eliminate the word "eyes" and touch your eyes.

When you start eliminating the words, go very slowly so everyone can keep up with you. After the children are familiar with the words and actions, you can say it faster and faster—this is really fun!

Chant:

My [touch your chest] *face* [touch your face] it has *two* [hold up two fingers] *eyes* [touch eyes].
Two [hold up two fingers] *eyes* [touch your eyes] has *my* [touch your chest] *face* [touch your face].
And had it not *two* [hold up two fingers] *eyes* [touch your eyes],
It would not be *my* [touch your chest] *face* [touch your face].

Variations:

1. Provide four different instruments, one for each italicized word: My, face, two, eyes. Have four children or four groups of children play on the eliminated words while the rest of the class says the chant and does the actions.

2. Can also be sung to the tune, "My Hat It Has Three Corners."

Number Chant

Rita Shotwell

Ages: 5–9 years

Materials: Bells and wood sounding instruments (rhythm sticks, castanets, wood blocks) for variations

Chant:

> One, two, there's a bug on you.
> Three, four, there's a spider on the door.
> Five, six, there's an insect on the stick.
> Seven, eight, they're all on the gate.
> Nine, ten, they've fallen again.

Directions: Say the chant and pat your thighs two times on the numbers and clap three times on the rhyme.

Divide the class into two groups and:

Group 1: pat thighs two times while saying the numbers.

Group 2: clap three times while saying the rhyme.

Reverse the groups and repeat the chant.

Extend: Take a partner. Sit on the floor, facing your partner and pat your thighs on the numbers and clap your partner's hands on the rhyme.

Variation #1:

Use rhythm instruments. Have the wood sounds play on the numbers and the bells play on the rhyme. Reverse, have the bells play on the numbers and the wood sounds on the rhyme.

Variation #2:

Have the wood sounds play two taps on the numbers and have the bells play the *rhythm of the words* on the rhyme. Reverse and have the bells play the numbers and the wood sounds play the rhythm of the words on the rhyme.

Wigalee, Swigalee

Rita Shotwell

Ages: 3–6 years

Directions: Children hold their thumbs out in front and keep moving them up and down, while the teacher (or leader) says the chant. The last word is "me." On this signal the teacher arranges his/her thumbs in any position, which the children immediately imitate. (Example, thumbs point down.)

Chant:

Wigalee, swigalee
Wigalee, swee,
Look at my *thumbs*,
Look at *me*!

Next, the chant is repeated but this time all ten fingers are wiggled until the signal word "me." Then the leader arranges fingers in any interesting way and the children imitate as quickly as possible. (Example: place hands on either side of the forehead with fingers extended out to the side, thumbs touching temples.)

Other variations of body parts and actions:

hands—cup hands around ears at the end of the rhyme

arms—spread arms out to the side at the end of the rhyme

shoulders—lift shoulders up to ears at the end of the rhyme

head—bow head down at the end of the rhyme

Comments: Children can take turns being the leader. Other body parts and actions can be added. In this game, children listen for the cue word and react quickly. They increase body awareness. This is a good relaxation game because you are exercising individual body parts.

You could end the game with, "look at my *body*, look at me" and freeze into a funny looking statue.

Wiggle, Waggle

Rita Shotwell

Ages: 4–9 years

Directions: Say the chant through once, with actions, for the students. Have the children echo each line as you say it again: include actions. Say the chant four times:

First time—speak in a normal tone.

Second time—speak a little softer.

Third time—whisper words.

Fourth time—"think" the words but do the actions.

Chant:

My arms go *up* [Raise arms up in the air.]
My arms go *down* [Lower arms to side of body.]
My arms go *round* and *round* and *round* [Roll arms one over the other three times.]
My fingers go *snap* [Raise arms up in the air and snap fingers.]
My toes go *tap* [Lean back on heels and tap ground with toes, both feet at same time.]
My body goes *wiggle waggle* [Shake whole body.]
Just like *that*! [Stamp foot and punch the air in front of you.]

Variation #1: Say the chant three times:

First time—speak in normal voice.

Second time—hum the words.

Third time—"think" words, do actions.

Variation #2: Add instruments:

Finger cymbals or triangle on the word, "up"

Tone Block on the word, "down"

Maracas on the word, "round" (one shake each time)

Bells on the word, "snap" (one shake)

Castanets on the word, "tap"

Tambourine on the words, "wiggle-waggle" (one long shake)

Hand Drum and mallet on the word, "that"

Comments: This activity provides the following benefits: concentration (waiting for cues), coordination of words with actions, and practice with instruments.

Fuzzy Wuzzy

Ages: 2–4 years

Directions: The teacher sits in front of the group to demonstrate and sing the song. Ask children to listen and watch carefully. The teacher uses a tickling motion on the head, the chin, and the tummy as high, middle, and low notes are sung respectively. Have children sing and tickle with you—noting that high sounds are on the head, middle sounds are on the chin, and low notes are on the "tummy."

(To help simplify this, there are initials for head (H), Chin (C) and tummy (T) above the notation.)

Variations:

Ask for a volunteer from the group to come sit on your lap. As the song is sung, the teacher tickles the head, chin, and tummy of the volunteer child who should try to stay very serious.

Comments: If done gently, this game can be both amusing and affectionate. It is very popular with young children.

Hoo-Ray for Angie

Ages: 2–5 years

Directions: Children may sing this simple song during circle time, while waiting for anything (for example, the school bus), or it may be used during transition times.

Variations:

Change the words to: "*What* do we appreciate?" Lunch, music, swimming, game time, a visitor.

Comments: This little song helps children practice social give and take, and it builds self-esteem.

Humpty Dumpty

Ages: 2–4 years

Directions: This little game can be a fingergame or a fingergame-song. Motions follow below:

HUMP-TY DUMP-TY SAT ON A WALL, HUMP-TY DUMP-TY HAD A GREAT FALL

ONE FIST ON TOP OF OTHER

FIST FALLS DOWN

ALL THE KING'S HOR-SES AND ALL THE KING'S MEN

WALK FOUR FINGER

WALK TWO FINGERS

COULD-N'T PUT HUMP-TY TO-GE-THER A-GAIN.

SHAKE HEAD & WAGGLE POINTERFINGER

Comments: Ask the children why we use four fingers to represent the horses and two fingers to represent the men; and why they couldn't put Humpty-Dumpty, the egg, back together again.

Jack and Jill

(New Version)

Ages: 4–5 years

Directions: Learn the rhyme first. Then add hand motions below as a finger game. Better still, see what gestures and motions the children can come up with.

JACK AND JILL WENT UP THE HILL, TO FETCH A PAIL OF WA-TER
(CLIMB FISTS HAND OVER HAND) · · · ·

JACK FELL DOWN, AND BROKE HIS CROWN, AND JILL CAME TUM-BLING AF-TER.
(ONE FIST DROPS DOWN)   (OTHER FIST DROPS DOWN)

Verse 2:

Up Jack got, and picked up Jill [slowly form arms into a cradle]
And in his arms he held her [rock cradle]
"You're not hurt: brush off the dirt [brush hands],
Let's go and fetch the water."

Verse 3:

So Jack and Jill went up the hill [slow climbing motions]
To fetch a pail of water
Brought it back to Mother Dear [climb hands downwards]
Who thanked her son [one hand out] and daughter [other hand out].

Alternate verse 2 (traditional):

Up Jack got and home did trot,
As fast as he could caper.
Went to bed, to mend his head,
With vinegar and brown paper.

Variation: Later in the year children could act out the motions with their whole bodies: stepping up with legs, Jill falls down, Jack helps her up and brushes her off, they bring the water to the teacher (Mother).

Comments: Discuss with the children the meanings of some of the unusual words and expressions in the verse (broke his crown, fetch, caper, etc.).

Jack Be Nimble

(Can Be a Chant or a Song)

Ages: 3–5 years

Directions: As the song is sung and repeated quickly around the circle, each child gets a turn jumping over the candlestick (a block or real **unlit** candle). Use each child's name instead of Jack. Tell the child to pretend her feet are tied or glued together.

BAR-BARA BE NIM-BLE, BAR-BARA BE QUICK

BAR-BARA JUMP O-VER THE CAN-DLE-STICK.

Comments: You can get a lot of turns in, in a short time. As you go around the circle, there is pleasant anticipation as each child waits for a turn. They know who's coming next and can get ready. For a variation, each child can pick the next one to have a turn.

A Little Boy (Girl) Went Walking By

Ages: 2–5 years

Directions: The whole group sings the first two lines of the song, and a designated child sings the next two lines (the response). If the child is too young or too shy to sing the response, the group can sing that part too.

A LIT-TLE BOY WENT WALK-ING BY, WALK-ING BY, WALK-ING BY A

LIT-TLE BOY WENT WALK-ING BY, WHO ARE YOU? HIS (MY)

NAME IS RON-ALD MATT-I-SON, MATT-I-SON, MATT-I-SON. HIS (MY)

NAME IS RON-ALD MATT-I-SON HOW DO YOU DO?

Comments: The song can be sung while children are seated in a circle, or at the lunch table, while waiting for anything, or as a transition (for example, as children pick up toys and prepare for another activity). It may help children learn each other's names at the beginning of the school year. The child may sing the response, or the whole group may sing it.

Tickle, Tickle, Bumble Bee

Ages: 2–4 years

Directions: The children sit in a circle. The teacher kneels beside each child in turn, tickles him or her on the arm *very* gently, and sings the question below. The child, and then the class, answer.

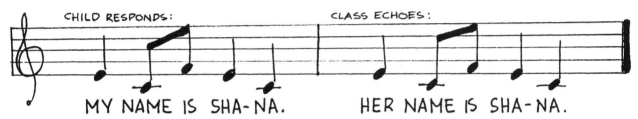

Comments: If a child is too shy to sing a response, it is fine if she just speaks her name (or even whispers it).

In order to get around the circle quickly, each verse should follow immediately after the previous one.

This song provides an opportunity for the group to focus attention briefly on each child.

Yankee Doodle

Ages: 3 to 6 years

Directions: Everyone is seated in a circle. Teacher sings the song once with actions:

[Line 1] Yankee Doodle went to town a-riding on a pony
[Pat thighs 8 times while singing.]

[Line 2] Stuck a feather in his hat and called it "macaroni"
[Extend arms out and draw back four times while singing.]

[Line 3] Yankee Doodle keep it up, Yankee Doodle dandy
[Roll arms, one over the other, eight times.]

[Line 4] Mind the music and the step and with the girls be handy.
[Continue to roll arms, one over the other eight more times.]

Repeat the song and actions and have children join in.

Variation #1: Everyone standing:

Line 1—March *in place* eight steps.

Line 2—Stand in place and do four knee bends.

Line 3 & 4—Run *in place* 16 steps.

Variation #2:

March around the room on line 1.

Stand in place and do knee bends on line 2.

Take a partner and gallop around the room on lines 3 and 4.

Repeat the song getting a new partner each time.

Sing the song four times so children will have four different partners.

Variation #3:

Children stand in a circle. The teacher explains that this time they will sing the song and do the above actions (Variation #2), but they all have to be back to the circle at the end of the song.

To make sure everyone gets back to the circle by the end of the song, tell the children to start coming back to the circle at the beginning of line 4, "Mind the music, etc."

4

SCIENCE and NATURE

In an extended-day program, it is sometimes possible to give children learning experiences they may never have had and may never have again. For example, building an incubator and hatching eggs can be an experience that will never be forgotten.

Science and nature projects like the incubator may extend over a few or many days. A number of other projects in this chapter, such as rooting plants, simple constructions of wood, a crystal garden, and growing sprouts, will provide hours of interesting things to do and watch.

A set of musical instruments can be made over a period of days or weeks, but can be enjoyed all year long. (Use these homemade instruments with some of the songs and fingergames found in Chapter 3.) Each child may wish to make a separate set of instruments to take home.

Most children like to know "how things work" and "why things happen." This section explores some of the marvels that exist in everyday life.

Constructing a Cold Frame

(A Homemade Greenhouse)

Ages: 4 years and up. Younger children will enjoy the planting and growing process. Older children can assist in building the frame. **With adult supervision.**

Materials & Equipment:
Two pieces of wood 2 × 12 inches × 5 feet

Two pieces of wood 2 × 12 inches × 3 feet

Nails

Hammer

Thick clear plastic sheeting (dropcloths) big enough to cover the box and overhang on the ground to be anchored down

Shallow (2–3 inches deep) containers that can have holes punched in their bottoms, or inexpensive plastic flats available at nurseries or garden suppliers

Potting soil

Sand

Flower and vegetable seeds, such as radishes or marigolds, that germinate quickly.

Large stones, bricks, or heavy boards to anchor the plastic sheeting to the ground

Directions: A cold frame is a bottomless box covered by a plastic sheet that uses the sun's heat to warm its enclosed area. Using a cold frame allows you to start seeds outside before you can actually plant them in a garden.

Assemble the four pieces of wood into a rectangle 3 × 5 feet. Nail the pieces together at the corners and set the frame up on a flat piece of ground on the south side of your property. Try to back it up to a hedge, a fence, or a building. Don't choose a spot where water pools after a rain storm. Dump in a 2-inch layer of sand and spread it evenly around in the frame.

Prepare the shallow growing containers or flats by filling them with potting soil. Gently press the soil down. It is important to remember that these containers must have drainage holes in the bottom. Make shallow trenches in the soil every three inches across the width of the flat and drop in your seeds. Cover seeds with soil to the depth recommended on the seed package. Label each of the rows so you won't forget what you have planted. Moisten the soil carefully, and keep it moist at all times.

Move the newly planted flats out to the cold frame box. When all the flats have been arranged inside the area, cover the frame with the large piece of clear heavy plastic sheeting. Anchor the plastic sheet down with heavy boards, bricks or stones on all four sides. You will need to check often to see if the soil in the flats is moist, and on very hot days you will have to prop open the plastic sheeting a bit to permit some air to circulate within the box.

In many sections of the country, this makes a good early spring activity.

When the seeds begin to sprout, watch them carefully. You don't want them to be overcrowded. If this happens thin them out by moving some to other containers, or if you have plenty, discard the extras. A tongue depresser can be used to lift the plant gently out of the soil and into another container.

When all danger of frost has left the area, the plants are ready to transplant to a garden spot.

Children can take the plants home in a soil-filled styrofoam cup, or use the plants to make a garden together.

Dried Flowers and Leaves

Ages: 5 years and up

Method I—Pressing

Materials & Equipment: Cut flowers from the garden
Wild flowers from fields or roadsides
Leaves from different trees
Old newspapers
Roll of soft paper towels
Old phone books, large mail order catalogs
Heavy books, bricks, or stones

Directions: The flowers or leaves should be picked or gathered the day you plan to press them into books. Divide the pages of either an old phone book or a large catalog into three equal sections, and place a layer of newspaper with a layer of paper towels on top at each of the dividing points. Place the flower or leaf specimens carefully on the paper towel in each section and cover them with another layer of paper towel and newspaper. Close the pages slowly and add more books, a brick, or a stone on top of the phone book or catalog to weigh down the pages even more effectively. Store in a dark, dry place for three to four weeks.

Method II—Borax Drying Method

**Materials
& Equipment:** Sand

Household laundry borax (amount will depend on how many flowers are to
be dried)

Medium-sized cardboard box with cover removed (size will depend on the
number of flowers to be dried)

Directions: Make a mixture of sand and borax—3 parts borax to 1 part sand.

Dump this mixture into the cardboard box and spread evenly.

Place each flower head face down in the borax mixture, making sure
that it is fully covered. You must use much care in handling the flowers
while doing this. Stems can be left uncovered and upright.

Leaves and flowers that need to be lying down in order to be covered
can be placed horizontally in the mixture.

Store in a dark, dry place for two to three weeks.

Comments: The dried flowers or leaves that have been pressed can be used to make pictures which can be framed. They also make handsome book marks. The
flowers or leaves could also be mounted on a large poster and labeled as a
project in flower or tree identification. White glue is all you need to attach
these dried plants to a background material. Very gentle handling must also
be encouraged. Pictures may be covered with glass and frame, or plastic
wrap.

Since you would obtain three-dimensional dried flowers with the borax
drying method, the children might make their own floral and leaf arrange-
ments in small clay pots filled with floral foam or sand.

Recycled Paper

Ages: 6–10 years

Materials & Equipment: Old or used paper, especially newsprint or paper bags

Piece of screen about 6 inches square for each child. Rough edges can be covered with duct tape.

Plastic dish pan that is somewhat wider than the screen pieces

More newspapers for blotting

Bowl for mixing

Egg beater or electric blender. **Use of a blender should be supervised.**

Rolling pin or wooden dowel or sponge

Green leaves

Directions:

1. Tear the used paper into little tiny pieces; the smaller, the better (½-inch square or smaller).
2. Fill a bowl or a blender three-quarters full with hot water.
3. Add one handful of torn paper and six small green leaves (rather soft leaves, as from a shrub).
4. Beat or blend together until pulpy. If using a blender, make sure the lid is on when blending; use plenty of water to blend faster and to reduce strain on blender; turn off blender when it seems to be working too hard and add more water.
5. Pour the pulp into the plastic dishpan.
6. Slide the screen into the bottom of the pan and move it around until it is evenly coated with pulp—about ⅜-inches thick is a good covering. Watch out for thin spots.
7. Lift the screen out carefully, holding it level while it drains.
8. Put the screen, pulp side up, on the blotting newspaper. Put more newspaper on top of the screen and use a rolling pin, dowel or sponge to remove excess moisture.
9. Carefully remove the top newspaper and move the screen with the pulp to some more dry newspaper where it can be left to dry.
10. When the paper is almost dry you can peel it off the screen. Let it then dry completely. Evaporation of all of the moisture takes about 2 days.
11. As the children continue to make paper you use up much of the pulp and the slurry (as it is called) gets more and more watery. Keep adding pulp to maintain the desired consistency.

Comments: This is a winner! Every child is excited when the process really works. The recycled paper can be used to make the children's own books or special holiday cards.

This project naturally leads into a discussion of environmental concerns, and the way paper is made.

Growing Sprouts

Age: All ages

Materials & Equipment: A collection of small- or medium-sized glass jars

Old nylon stockings that can be cut up to use as covers; the sprouts need some air circulation

Rubber bands to attach nylon stocking to top of jar

Ingredients: Alfalfa seeds

Directions: Have the children fill their jars ⅛ to ¼ full of seeds. Cover the seeds with warm water and soak overnight. The next day, drain the seeds well and cover the top of the jar with a piece of nylon stocking secured by a rubber band.

Place the jars somewhere in the room that is not in direct sunlight.

For the next three or four days, the seeds must be rinsed and drained twice daily, morning and late afternoon or evening.

When the seeds begin to sprout, place the jars in direct sunlight so they will green up.

Store sprouts in the refrigerator after they become green. They can be kept fresh like this for about two weeks.

Serve in sandwiches as a topping, on crackers that have been spread with cream cheese, or in a "little of everything" salad.

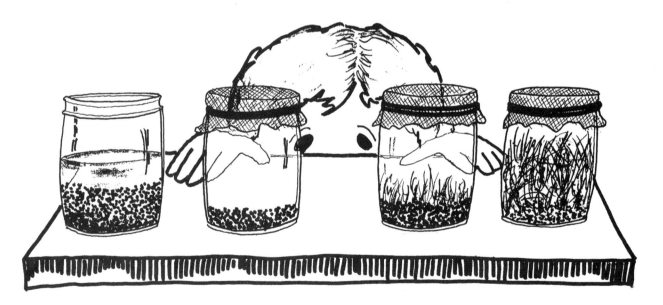

Rooting Plants

Ages: 4 years and up

Materials & Equipment: Stem cuttings from common house plants such as coleus, wandering jew, or philodendron

Runners from an airplane spider plant

Small glasses or jars

Potting soil

Paper or styrofoam cups; used small clay pots

Sharp knife *(Used with supervision)*

Directions: Stem cuttings should be at least five to six inches long and have four to six leaves on them. Select a mature stem (not a fairly new one) and with the sharp knife cut just below a point where a leaf joins the stem. Strip off the bottom leaves so that only the stem will be immersed in water. Put the cuttings in small jars or glasses filled with water and place them in the room where there is indirect light.

When several roots appear dangling in the water, remove the cuttings from the water and pot them in containers (paper or styrofoam cups, used clay pots) that have been half-filled with potting soil. Carefully add more potting soil and press down lightly so that the fragile new roots will not be broken off. Moisten the soil with some water when you have finished.

If you use styrofoam cups to pot the new plants, you will eventually have to repot them into regular plant containers. Potting several baby plants into a larger pot can also be done.

Runners are long stems sent out by a plant with little new plants at the end of them. Airplane (spider) plants are the most common house plant that propagates in this fashion. Cut off the plantlets, root them in water and then pot them in small containers or clay pots just as you do for stem cuttings.

Comments: Plants are a wonderful addition to any environment. Rooting and watching baby plants grow gives added pleasure to having plants around you. Plants also make nice gifts.

Cuttings can be obtained from people who have house plants or from the ones in your own surroundings. The only expense involved is purchasing good potting soil.

Building an Incubator and Hatching Eggs

Ages: This activity can involve children of many different ages. Older children can be involved in the actual construction of the incubator and brooder box; in the tasks of turning the eggs; and checking, maintaining, and recording the temperature. Younger children may help in turning eggs, but will learn primarily from watching the preparations and the miracle of birth.

Supplies: One dozen fertile eggs—can be obtained from hatcheries, poultry breeding farms, or sometimes from university extension services

Incubator—can be purchased, or make one from directions which follow.

Pan of water

Two thermometers (accurate to 103° Fahrenheit)

Brooder Box (directions follow incubator directions)

To Make Incubator:

Equipment & Materials: One cardboard box about 18 × 18 × 18 inches

One cardboard box about 16 × 16 × 16 inches

Crumpled paper or old cloth for insulation

Light bulb on a cord

Light bulbs of various wattages

Newspapers

Thermometer (accurate to 103°F)

Plastic transparent material

Small knife

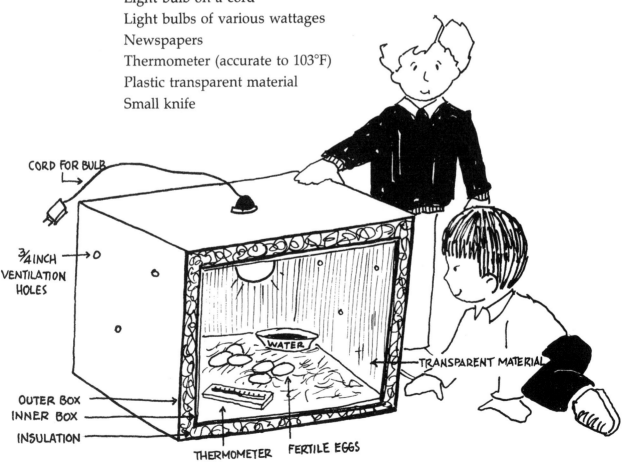

CORD FOR BULB

¾ INCH VENTILATION HOLES

TRANSPARENT MATERIAL

WATER

OUTER BOX
INNER BOX
INSULATION

THERMOMETER   FERTILE EGGS

Directions for making incubator:

(The incubator should be constructed in advance of obtaining the fertile eggs so that there will be time for adjusting the temperature properly.)

Turn the boxes on their sides; put the smaller box inside the larger one, packing the insulating material between them. Line the floor of the inner box with newspapers.

Make a small opening in the "ceiling" of the box and suspend the light bulb inside the box. Place the thermometer on the floor of the box, away from the light bulb. Attach the transparent material to the open front, like a window, so that the transparent material can be removed to change the light bulb. (Tape it and retape it each time you put the "window" back. **An adult should monitor the bulbs used and their correct installation.**

Test bulbs of different wattage until you find one that keeps the box temperature at 102°F–103°F for an entire day. If the box gets too hot you can punch two or three ¾-inch ventilation holes on two sides of the box, and make paper plugs to fit them. By removing the plugs you can cool the box if it gets a little too warm.

Put the dozen fertile eggs in the incubator. Mark the eggs on one of their sides with a pencil. Turn the eggs twice daily at 12-hour intervals for the first ten days. Note the pencil marks so you'll know which have been turned. Eggs should lie on their sides with the large end raised slightly. The smaller end should never be higher than the large end. Keep a record of the time of turning and the temperature of the box each time you turn the eggs.

Keep a pan of water in the incubator. The surface of the water should be as large as the eggs bunched together would be. The most common fault in homemade incubators is too much ventilation and too little moisture.

Do not turn the eggs after the eighteenth day of incubation and do not open the incubator except to add warm water. Watch the temperature carefully. Check often, three times each day. On the nineteenth day, some eggs will hatch; on the twentieth day, many should hatch. On the twenty-first day add boiling water to the water pan to steam up the incubator and help hatch any remaining unhatched eggs.

After the chicks hatch, wait until they are fully dry and fluffy before removing them to the brooder box. (Directions for making the brooder box are on the next page.) Then give them water and food (chick mash). Plans for permanent placement of the chicks should be made before starting this project. If the source for your fertile eggs doesn't provide this information, the local humane society can be very helpful.

Let children touch the chicks' down very gently. It is much preferred that children do not hold chicks. It is the miracle of seeing the chick's birth, and seeing them walking around in their incubator and then in the brooding box, that constitutes the real pleasure of this project.

Children should not be given chicks to take home unless there is absolute certainty that the chicks can be cared for properly.

Brooder Box

(Temporary One for Holding Chicks for One or Two Days)

Materials & Equipment: Large cardboard box without a top (Sides should be high enough so chicks can't get out.)

Gooseneck lamp, adjustable lamp or hanging bulb that can be turned on as needed to keep the box warm

Thermometer to check the temperature of the box (90°F)

Food tray—metal covers from large food jars with some depth to the rims

Water tray (flat) lined with marbles so the chicks won't drown; or a special self-feeding water jar for chicks, available at hatcheries.

Old newspapers

Mash (chick feed). Mash to feed the chicks should be available at the place you obtain the fertile eggs. Extension services at local state universities often have materials available on poultry projects, also.

Directions: Suspend a hanging bulb or adjust a gooseneck or other flexible lamp so that the heat from the bulb will warm the brooder box to about 90°F. The temperature of the brooder box should be kept as near as possible to 90°F.

Attach the thermometer to a side of the box, away from the bulb. Line the box with old newspapers. Provide clean water in a large lid or flat water tray lined with marbles to prevent the chicks from falling in, and/or use a continuous feed, upside-down water jar. Clean water must be available at all times. **Lamp and water should never come in contact.** Place mash (chick feed) in feeder tray.

Newspaper liner in the box should be changed often.

Keep the food and water trays well supplied.

Chicks should be thoroughly dry and fluffed before transferring to the brooder.

Floating Egg

Ages: 5–10 years

Benefits: An easy and interesting experiment that teaches beginning concepts (for older children) of solutions, saturated solutions, and density.

Materials & Equipment: one 2-quart pan
two 1-quart (or larger) glass jars
One box of salt
A source of heat (stove or hot plate) **Used only by an adult.**
Two or three large spoons

Directions: Using a 2-quart pan (a flameproof glass one is ideal), first prepare the saturated solution. Keep adding salt to a quart of boiling water and stir until the water will not take up any more salt. Add water to keep it at the 1-quart level. Let children take turns stirring the solution, emphasizing safety.

After hot solution has cooled, prepare two jars: (1) with plain water and (2) with the cool saturated solution. Carefully place a (raw) egg, in its shell, into the jar of plain water. It will sink. The egg is more dense than the water, therefore it sinks.

Now, place the same or another egg into the saturated salt solution. This solution is more dense than the egg. The egg will float.

Children will learn from the experiment even though they may not understand the concept of density.

Comments: **Have a dishpan full of cold water available. In case any child gets burned, plunge the burned area into the cold water immediately.** With careful supervision and careful placement of the pan on the burner, there should be no danger.

There are two more experiments you can do with the leftover concentrated salt solution, Salt Crystals and Chemical Garden, on the following pages.

Salt Crystals

Ages: 6–10 years. Some younger children may be interested.

Benefits: Children observe how liquids may change to solids and how crystals develop.

Materials & Equipment: After doing the experiment Floating Egg, you will have at least two cups of saturated salt solution. Or you can make a saturated salt solution by pouring salt into a quart of boiling water and stirring it until no more salt will dissolve. **(Adult supervision)**

    Each child needs a glass jar, preferably five or six inches deep, pieces of string, a large nail or straw to hold the string, and a paper clip or small nail at the bottom end of the string.

Directions: Suspend a wet cotton string into the saturated salt solution. A long nail across the top of the jar will hold the string in a vertical position, and a paper clip or small nail at the other end will keep the string from floating.

    Within a day or two, salt crystals should begin to form along the string.

Variation: You can do this with a sugar solution and "grow" rock candy.

Chemical Garden

(Depression Plant)

Ages: 4–10 years

Benefits: To observe crystals "growing" on coal or brick.

**Materials
& Equipment:**
Coal, or pieces of brick charcoal
Salt (concentrated solution)—see comments
Ammonia
Clothes bluing, ink, or food coloring
Large glass bowl

Directions:
1. Arrange pieces of coal (or brick) in a bowl, large if possible.
2. Add 1 T. ammonia to one or two cups of the salt solution.
3. Pour the saturated salt solution over the pieces of coal.
4. Put a few drops of bluing, red & blue food coloring, or ink onto the coal.

Move the bowl to a place of easy visibility where it need not be moved again. In a day or two, white and colored crystals will grow on the coal and edges of the dish. Look at the crystals with a magnifying glass. Children may want to take the recipe for a chemical garden home with them, to grow their own crystals.

Comments: To make a saturated salt solution, stir salt into two cups very hot or boiling water until no more salt will dissolve. **Adult supervision.**

Bird Feeders

Easy, school-made bird feeders come in many forms, including the following:

1. Simple wooden trays or tray-like boxes which children can make. These can be filled with various types of food or seed, described below.
2. A variety of dispensers can be filled with a mixture of melted suet and bird seed or other dry ingredients.
3. Strings of popcorn, cranberries, or other foods enjoyed by birds may easily be made with a large-eyed needle and strong thread.

Equipment: Meat grinder to grind the suet

Double boiler to melt suet

Large bowl and fork or spoon to mix ingredients

Large needles and heavy thread for stringing bird foods

As desired: Loaf or cake pans to mold suet (for solid blocks); coconut shells; pine cones; net bags, wire baskets; small logs with holes at various points.

Grinder and double boiler must be supervised by adult.

Ingredients: Raw beef suet

Sand or bird gravel

Kitchen scraps: leftover cake, doughnuts, cookies, stale bread, crusts, etc.

Thistle, millet, sunflower seeds; cracked corn, peanut hearts, and/or wild bird seed.

(1) Ground feeders:

Directions: The so-called ground feeder type of bird seed dispenser may be made of castoff pieces of wood (from your local lumberyard) shaped into simple shallow boxes. A tray-type dispenser may be made from a flat piece of wood with a little molding around the edge to hold the seed. Shallow plastic containers (a cut-off bleach bottle) are also suitable. In all cases, a few drainage holes should be drilled in the bottom of the box or tray. A little grit in the form of bird gravel or clean sand should be added periodically in the ratio of ½ teaspoon gravel to 1 cup of birdseed.

Several seed dispensers may be used in order to attract different kinds of birds. One dispenser could contain wild bird seed; another sunflower seeds; and a third, thistle seeds. Cardinals especially love sunflower seeds and finches are fond of thistle seeds.

(2) Suet dispensers:

Directions: **First, set up the pan and heater for melting the suet with safety well in mind.** For all the suet dispensers to be described, the suet must be put through a meat grinder, melted down, cooled a bit, and then reheated and poured into a loaf pan or over the dry ingredients while still in liquid form.

A half-teaspoon of bird gravel or sand should always be added to each cup of dry mixture to help birds digest the coarse foods they eat. Experiment with different mixtures of dry ingredients (see Ingredients list). Add enough melted suet to hold the mixture together and mix well.

SUET-STUFFED LOG

COCONUT SHELL

a. The children can mold a suet mixture in a loaf pan, refrigerate until firm and then place on a ground feeder. The hardened block can also be cut in pieces, placed in a plastic-coated wire basket and hung on a tree limb, or placed in pieces on a tray feeder.

b. Children can take pine cones with strings or wire attached, *spoon the warm suet over them*, sprinkle with bird seed, push in some sunflower seeds, and spoon some more suet over the cones again to hold the dry food securely. Refrigerate until firm and hang outside.

c. Partially fill half a coconut shell with dry ingredients plus ½ teaspoon sand. After heating the suet twice, pour some of the hot liquid over the dry ingredients in the shell and put in the refrigerator to harden. Hang from a tree branch.

d. In a large bowl, combine some dry ingredients and some sand for grit. Add the warm, melted suet and mix until dry foods are well covered. Turn out onto a large piece of waxed paper. Bring the paper up around the suet mixture, pressing into the shape of a ball. Refrigerate and then put the ball in a net bag and suspend from a branch of a tree.

e. To attract woodpeckers, drill large holes at various points into small wooden logs, and fill with a mixture of melted suet and dry seed or scraps of bread, etc. Don't forget the small pinch of gravel or sand each time. Add wire or string and hang from a tree branch.

(3) String Feeders:

Directions: Children can string such foods as popcorn, raisins, cranberries, pieces of doughnut or bread, peanuts-in-the-shell, etc. for the birds to eat. These strings are especially attractive on evergreen trees, providing the birds with food and a snug, secure place to perch. A large-eyed needle and strong thread for each child is all that is needed, in addition to the food to be strung.

Making Musical Instruments

Making musical instruments can be a scientific experiment, an art or craft project, or a way to enrich a musical game or song. It could be a single activity or a long-term plan. It could involve mixed ages easily, for the older children could do the more difficult tasks.

If a variety of instruments are made they can be a source of ongoing pleasure for plain exploration or organized musical events.

Whenever the project of making a musical instrument is planned, it is important to have all the materials on hand and clear visual instructions available, if possible.

The water bells and flower pots provide melody or pitched sounds.

The drums and tub bass provide a strong beat to hold the group together.

The other percussive sounds provide variety through different timbres.

With just a little guidance from an adult at the beginning, a group of children can then take over and "do their own thing."

They can accompany well-known pop songs on records or in group singing.

Flowerpot Bells

Ages: 5 years and up

Materials & Equipment: Clean, unglazed clay flowerpots of many different sizes
Cord or heavy string
A broomstick or other sturdy stick from which to hang the flowerpots
Different size pieces of thin dowel
Pencils or thin dowels with which to strike the bells

Directions: Choose a piece of dowel that will fit on the bottom of each flowerpot. Knot a different length of cord around each piece and thread the string through the hole in the bottom of the flowerpot from the inside to the outside. Hang them all from a broomstick or some such support. The pots must not touch each other—that is the reason for the different lengths of cord. Strike the pots lightly with a pencil or thin stick—they are fragile and crack easily. Hang the pot with the deepest sound on the left, and the highest sound on the right.

Comments: It is difficult to tune flowerpots, but it can be done, at least from low to high sounds. Generally the children will enjoy the variety of sounds and not try to play a specific tune. Perhaps they can sing "Twinkle, Twinkle, Little Star" to an entirely new, original tune.

Children will be able to explore sounds, and learn something of the relationship of size with sound. Perhaps they will be able to match the various tones with their voices.

Water Bells

Ages: 5 years and up can play the bells with numbers.

Preschool children can enjoy the bells without trying to play a melody.

Equipment: Water and drinking glasses or any glass containers (of same or different sizes). The containers should have a clear ringing sound when you strike them with a pencil or wooden dowel. Many different containers are needed to get a good range of sounds.

Directions: Experiment by pouring different levels of water into all the drinking glasses (or other glass containers). With patience, you can make a musical scale and be able to play simple tunes of one octave, or make up your own songs. Line up the glasses with the lowest sounding glass on the left and the highest sounding on the right.

Mark the level of water on each glass with a piece of tape so that tuning won't be necessary each time you use the bells.

Twinkle, Twinkle, Little Star

$\frac{4}{4}$

1 1 5 5	6 6 5 ₹	4 4 3 3	2 2 1 ₹
5 5 4 4	3 3 2 ₹	5 5 4 4	3 3 2 ₹
1 1 5 5	6 6 5 ₹	4 4 3 3	2 2 1 ₹

Comments: Children will be able to explore sounds, recognize different pitches, and match the tones with their voices.

Hand Drums

Ages: 4–10 years

Materials & Equipment: Cardboard tubes, round cornmeal or oatmeal boxes

Coffee cans of different sizes

Any or all of the following can be used as "skins" for the drums:

>   rubber inner tubing
>
>   plastic jar or can tops
>
>   strong plastic sheeting
>
>   strong brown paper
>
>   burst balloons

Rubber bands—wide heavy ones—baling wire, and heavy twine

Scissors

Paint, contact paper, craft paper

Glue, crayons, markers, and other materials to decorate tubes, cereal boxes, or cans

Directions: Cardboard tube drums and cereal box drums:

1. Decorate the tubes or cereal boxes with colored paper, paint, crayons, or markers.

2. Cut circles (that are slightly larger than the tops of the boxes or tubes) out of heavy brown paper, plastic sheets, or burst balloons.

3. Stretch these "skins" over the top of each tube or cereal box and fasten the "skin" with a heavy rubber band. The tighter you can stretch the "skin," the better the sound. The tubes can be covered at both ends and the resulting drum can be hung around the child's neck so he can play it at both ends.

Coffee can drums:

1. Many coffee cans come with plastic covers to be used after they are opened. These plastic covers can serve as drum "skins."
2. Children may decorate the cans, add the plastic tops, and listen for the sounds that different-sized cans make.
3. Inner tubing makes a wonderful head for a coffee can drum. Cut a circular piece of rubber tubing slightly larger than the top of the can. Stretch it over the top of the can and attach it with baling wire.

   An even better sounding drum can be made by opening both ends of the coffee can, cutting two slightly larger pieces of inner tubing, stretching one over each end, and then lacing them together around the sides of the can. Use heavy twine to lace the two ends together after you have punched small holes at the appropriate places in the rubber tubing. These drums sound great and tend to have a longer life than other hand drums.

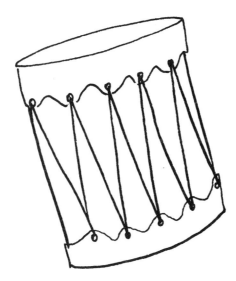

Comments: In making various types of drums, children will be experimenting with sounds as related to type and size of materials.

Rattles or Shakers

Ages: 4–10 years

Equipment: *(Containers):*
Paper cups with lids
Margarine containers with lids
Adhesive-bandage cans
Any other small plastic boxes or cans with covers
Tape to secure lids if they are not tight

Materials: Dried beans or peas
Rice
Sand
Salt
Seeds
Marbles
Small pebbles
Art materials to decorate the containers (optional)

Directions: Different containers will influence the sound that is made just as much as will the different contents.

Experiment with the variety of contents and containers listed above to find a variety of appealing combinations.

Remember that the materials inside the containers must be able to move about freely.

If the lids are not securely fastened when closed, apply some tape around the lid to prevent any accidental spilling of the contents.

TAPE LIDS TO AVOID SPILLS

Rhythm Sticks

Ages: 5–10 years

**Materials
& Equipment:** Pieces of doweling in different widths
Hand saw **(Use with adult supervision)**
Sandpaper (to smooth rough edges)
Paint or varnish to decorate sticks (optional)

Directions: Saw the pieces of doweling into different lengths so that you have pairs of sticks the same width and length: 6 to 12 inches is a good range of sizes. Sand them smooth and decorate them if you wish.

Rhythm sticks make the best sounds if tapped lightly. Holding one stick still while tapping the other on it make the sticks easier to handle. Try holding one stick across a cupped hand and tap it with the other one; see what kind of sound you get.

Sticks cut from broom handles and old chair legs make excellent musical instruments.

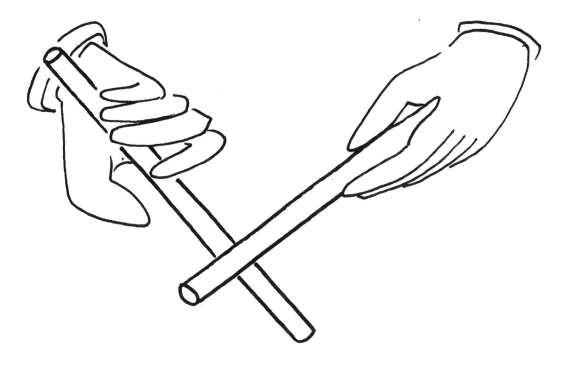

Comments: In this activity, children will not only enjoy using various simple woodworking tools, they will discover the sound properties of different lengths and widths of wood.

Sand Blocks

Ages: 4 years and up

Materials & Equipment: Small rectangular blocks (about 3 × 5 inches and ¾ inches thick, of soft wood
Sandpaper of different grades
Thumb tacks or large staple gun and staples
Empty spools and nails or wooden knobs and wood screws

Directions: Cut the sandpaper so that it will cover one wide surface and two sides of each block. Fasten it to the sides with thumb tacks or staples. For handles, nail the spools to the middle of the plain side of each block. If you use knobs, attach them with screws. **Staple gun and stapling should be handled by an adult.**

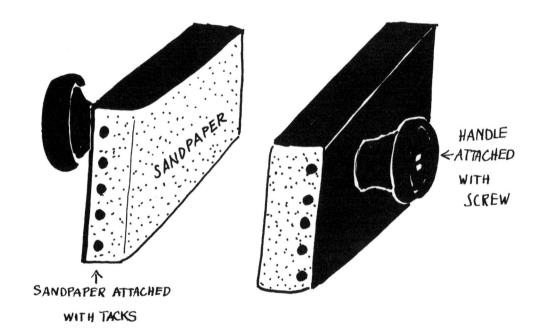

SANDPAPER ATTACHED
WITH TACKS

HANDLE
←ATTACHED
WITH
SCREW

Comments: The different grades of sandpaper will produce varying sounds. Sand blocks are especially good for the very young child. They are easy to play.
You might need washers to prevent the nail head from slipping into the hole of the spool.
The exploration of sounds and the recognition of percussion as a means of enhancing music are just two of the benefits of this activity.

Shoe Box Xylophone

Ages: 5 years and up

Materials & Equipment: Shoe boxes

Paper tubes (from waxed paper, paper towels, foil, plastic wrap, etc.)

The sturdier the tube, the better the sound.

Scissors and/or small sharp knife

Paint, crayons, markers, wallpaper pieces, glue, etc. to decorate box

Wooden stick about 12 inches long or a ruler (for use as a mallet in playing the xylophone)

Pencils

Directions: Place four or five of the paper tubes side by side on top of one shoe box. Decide how many will be able to fit, allowing some space on either side of each tube. Then with a pencil, mark both sides of the shoe box under each tube where you will then cut a notch for it to rest in. Proceed to cut these notches carefully with the scissors. The notch should not be more than ¾ inches deep.

At this point the shoe box can be decorated with paint, crayons, markers, wallpaper pieces, etc.

The next step is to cut the tubes into different lengths. (The sharp knife comes in handy at this time.)

Place the longest tube at the left side of the top of the box. The rest of the tubes are placed in order of size from the longest to the shortest. Decorate the tubes also; it strengthens them in the process.

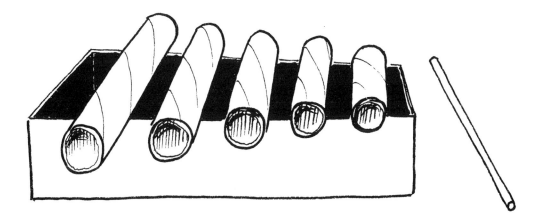

Comments: **Adult supervision is needed if you use the knife for cutting the tubes.** Other than this, children can handle this whole project on their own.

You will be surprised and pleased at the sound that this xylophone produces.

Children will experiment with the relationship between the length of the tube and the sound produced. They will also discover the purpose of a sound box.

Washtub Bass Fiddle

Ages: 5 years and up

Materials & Equipment:

Larger version:

A broomstick or other sturdy stick, such as a dowel, 30 inches in length

A hollow container, such as a metal washtub, metal wastebasket, or any very large tin can

Heavy string: nylon cord, thin clothesline, or bailing twine

Wooden peg or small piece of dowel, 1 to 2 inches long.

Tools: Saw, hammer, drill (hand or electric) with ¼-inch bit for drill. **Use these tools only with adult supervision.**

Smaller version:

One gallon cardboard paint bucket

30-inch length of dowel
or other stick, ¾ inches
or more in diameter

3 to 4 feet of heavy
string (bailing twine)

Wooden peg or small piece
of dowel 1 to 2 inches long

Directions: Drill a hole through one end of the stick about 1 inch from the end. In the other end saw a ⅛-inch groove down the middle of the end of the stick, about 1 inch long. (This groove will hold the lower edge of the stick in position on the rim of the tub or can or bucket.)

Then tie the small wooden peg or dowel securely to one end of the string. Punch a hole in the center of the bottom of the tub, can, or bucket (see comments below). Thread the string through the hole from inside to outside. The peg or dowel piece will keep one end of the string from slipping through the hole.

Next, thread the free end of the string through the hole in the stick and tie a large knot to hold it securely. The upright stick should hold the string taut. (see illustration).

Playing the washtub (tin can or paint bucket) bass:

Hook the grooved end of the stick over the rim of the tub, can, or bucket. Brace the tub (can or bucket) by putting one foot on the rim opposite the stick. Pull the stick toward you with one hand to tighten the string and pluck the string with the other hand.

The sound will be higher or lower as you tighten and loosen the tension on the string by moving the stick back and forth.

If you use your fingers to press the string against the stick at various places, you will also raise and lower the pitch of the sound.

Comments: When making the center hole (especially if using a cardboard paint bucket), make the hole small. The sound will be fuller if the hole is tight around the string. A small piece of wood under one edge of the tub will also improve the sound.

The bass fiddle provides a strong beat that holds a group of instruments or a group of voices together.

As a result of this project, children will become more familiar with different pitches, and will recognize a vibrating string as a source of sound and music.

Tambourine

Ages: 5 years and up

**Materials
& Equipment:** 6-inch blocks of wood cut from lengths of 1 × 2-inch boards

Bottle caps

Hammer and nails with wide heads **(use with adult supervision)**

Sandpaper (to smooth rough edges of wood)

Paint or markers (optional)

Directions: Remove the cork from the bottle caps. Hammer nails through the bottle caps so that the holes in the bottle caps are wide enough for the cap to slide freely along the nails. Sand each block of wood until it is smooth.

Using at least two caps on each nail, hammer the nail part way into one end of the wide side of the 6″ block of wood. Hammer two more sets of caps and nails directly below the first set.

Allow enough room for the block to be grasped as you play it.

Comments: This tambourine can be played by shaking it or by tapping the wooden side against your hand or knee. Tapping is usually easier for most children.

The tambourine can also be decorated with paint or markers.

5

HEALTHY SNACKS

The teacher may want to duplicate the recipes in this section, and let the older child manage on his/her own. Also, children enjoy taking the recipes home.

Some recipes (especially those requiring cooking) will require active supervision by an adult. Young children should not cook at the stove or hot plate but can participate in all other preparations.

Many teachers transfer the recipe to a large sheet of paper or poster board, to help children who don't yet read well. (Cooking is a good motivator for reading.)

Songs or fingergames are often fun to do while constructing snacks or while waiting for them to bake. Since much of the after school time is and should be spent in individual choice projects, snack time may be the one time when children get together.

Another idea is to put the materials out on a tray and let children make their own snacks and eat them a few at a time. One teacher we know calls this "loose juice time."

Ages are not specified in this section, as all ages of children can participate in at least part of the preparation of all the recipes.

Every cooking experience can be a mini natural science lesson, as children learn where the ingredients come from, how they change form during preparation, and how the materials contribute to nutrition. Children use arithmetic skills in measuring, and learn in a pleasurable way how to follow a sequence of directions. Snack preparation and snack eating time are wonderful times to learn social skills: cooperation, little courtesies and customs, having fun together.

Applesauce

(From Scratch)

Equipment: Large kettle with cover
Food mill or coarse strainer
Small kitchen knife

Ingredients: 8 large apples (about 3 lbs.)
Water
Sugar and cinnamon to taste

Directions: Wash, quarter, and remove the seeds of the 8 large apples. It is not necessary to peel apples. **Supervise the use of the knife.**

Immediately put the apples into a large kettle, add ½ cup water, cover, and simmer until apples are tender and mushy. Stir occasionally and add water in small amounts if needed.

Press apples through a food mill or coarse strainer.

Add small amounts of sugar and cinnamon to taste.

Yields: 16 servings

Comments: If children have also picked the apples, so much the better.

Try planting the seeds, and have a lot of patience waiting for them to sprout. One of the teachers at The Wilson School has the children plant orange, lemon, and apple seeds whenever the snacks include them. By the end of the year there are enough trees to send one home with each child.

Carrot and Raisin Salad

Equipment: Small hand grater
Vegetable peeler
Small knife
Small paper cups

Ingredients: Carrots
Raisins

Safety tips: **Grate and peel in motions away from the body. Supervise children using grater, peeler, and small knife.**

Directions: Most hand graters have at least two choices for grating foods. Choose the regular size, not the very fine. You want to end up with small, flat pieces (no chunks).

Prepare the carrots by washing and cutting off the two ends.
Scrape with a vegetable peeler and then grate into small pieces.
Add raisins to taste—probably ⅔ carrots and ⅓ raisins is a good mixture.
Serve individual portions in paper cups.

Crispy Vegetables and Dip

Equipment: Knife to cut up vegetables

Vegetable peeler

Bowl

Whisk or fork

Knife and peeler should be used with supervision.

Ingredients: Assortment of vegetables, such as:

Carrots, celery, broccoli, cauliflower, radishes, zucchini, cucumber, etc.

Commercial salad dressing dry mix that can be used as a dip. (Makes one pint.)

Milk—1 cup

Mayonnaise—1 cup

Directions:
1. Wash all vegetables and drain them.
2. Using a vegetable peeler, clean the carrots and celery and remove the skins of cucumbers (optional).
3. Break the cauliflower and broccoli into small flowerets (just big enough for one mouthful).
4. Cut the radishes in thick slices, the zucchini and cucumber in thin slices, and the carrots and celery into sticks.
5. Arrange on a platter, cover and chill.
6. Combine the commercial salad dressing mix, 1 cup milk, and 1 cup mayonnaise. Mix well with the wire whisk or a fork.

Refrigerate for at least 30 minutes to allow mix to thicken.
Stir before serving.

Comments: Using a milk and mayonnaise mixture for the dip instead of sour cream is not only less fattening but children like the taste better.

Crunchy Bananas

Equipment: Small tray or cookie sheet with edges all around
Small knife (optional)—**Use with supervision.**

Ingredients: Half a banana for each child (sliced horizontally)
Sesame seeds

Directions: Peel and break or cut each banana in half.
Sprinkle a fine coating of sesame seeds on the tray or cookie sheet.
Roll each banana half in the sesame seeds, pressing gently to make sure they stick.
Children can make this snack all on their own with an adult just supervising.

Fruit Kebobs

Equipment: Shish-kebob sticks (available at most big grocery stores)

Knife to cut up fruit—**use with supervision.**

Ingredients: Assorted fruits in season, such as:

Apples, pears, bananas, seedless grapes, oranges, melons, pineapple, plums, nectarines, peaches, etc. (Oranges should be the eating type, not juice ones.)

Lemon juice—to prevent discoloration of fruit.

Directions:

1. Wash and dry all fruit needing this attention. Peel the oranges and bananas, remove the rind and seeds from the melons, core the apples and pears, slice in half and pit the nectarines, peaches, and plums. Do not remove the skins from apples, pears and plums, or nectarines.

2. Save the seeds and pits from some of the fruit. You can try planting them and watch for the results.

3. Make plans to cut up all fruit so that the pieces are in bite-size chunks that can be placed on skewers without falling apart.

4. Place all cut-up pieces in a bowl and add a bit of lemon juice occasionally as you proceed to prevent some of the fruit from turning brown.

5. Children will enjoy placing the fruit on the skewer sticks. Make them as colorful and attractive as possible.

Orange Juice through a Peppermint Straw

Equipment: Apple corer or a small sharp knife—**use with supervision.**

Ingredients: Small juice oranges

Candy peppermint sticks, about 4 inches long

Directions: Roll each orange on a hard surface, pressing gently to soften the pulp and free the juices.

Using an apple corer or a sharp knife, make a cylindrical hole into the orange (from the end at which it is picked). Be careful not to go through the opposite end.

Pop in the peppermint stick and suck the juice just as you would through a straw.

Comments: A wonderful holiday treat! Juice oranges are least expensive at winter holiday time.

Blueberry Muffins

Equipment: Muffin pans with twelve 2½-inch cups

Large bowl

Large wooden spoon for mixing

Flour sifter

Shortening to grease tins, or paper cup liners

Ingredients: ¼ cup butter or margarine

2 cups sifted flour

⅓ cup sugar

1 tablespoon baking powder

½ teaspoon salt

1 egg (well-beaten)

1 cup milk

1 cup fresh or frozen blueberries

Directions: Melt and set aside to cool, ¼ cup of butter or margarine. **(Adult)**

Sift together into a bowl the 2 cups flour, ⅓ cup sugar, 1 tablespoon baking powder, and ½ teaspoon salt.

Make a well in the center of the dry ingredients and add the egg, which has been well beaten, and 1 cup of milk. Blend in the melted butter or margarine. With not more than a small number of strokes, quickly and lightly stir until the dry ingredients are barely moistened. The batter will be lumpy. Blueberries should be folded in quickly and gently during the final few strokes.

Fill each muffin cup two-thirds full.

Bake at 400°–425° (depending on oven) for 20–25 minutes. **(Adult)**

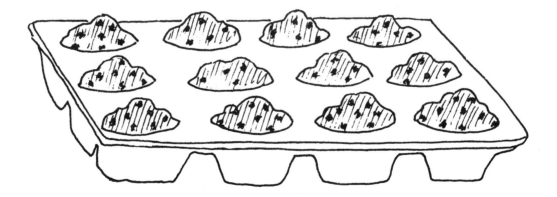

Comments: A cup of coarsely chopped cranberries mixed with 3 tablespoons of sugar can be substituted for the blueberries, or you could use both for a patriotic occasion.

Bran Muffins

Equipment: 2 medium-sized bowls

1 small pan

Muffin tin with twelve 2½-inch cups

Ingredients: 2 cups bran cereal (not flakes)

1¼ cups milk

1 cup all-purpose flour

⅓ cup firmly packed brown sugar

2 teaspoons baking powder

½ teaspoon baking soda

¼ cup (4 tablespoons) margarine, melted

1 egg, beaten

Directions: Combine bran and milk, let stand 5 minutes.

In the second bowl mix together the flour, the brown sugar, the baking powder, and the baking soda.

Melt the margarine in the small pan over low heat. **(Adult)**

Add the melted margarine and the beaten egg to the bran mixture.

Stir in the flour mixture just until blended.

Grease the muffin-pan cups and spoon the mixture evenly into the 12 cups.

Bake at 400° for 15–18 minutes. **(Adult)**

Serve warm or cooled.

Three-fourths cup of raisins can be added to the batter before cooking for an added good taste.

Cheese Krispies

Equipment: Pastry blender
Large bowl
Cookie sheets
Shortening to grease cookie sheets

Ingredients: 2 sticks margarine (softened)
2 cups flour, all-purpose
½ teaspoon salt
½ lb. grated sharp cheddar cheese
2 cups Rice Krispies
Dash of cayenne pepper

Directions: Mix all of the above ingredients, except the Rice Krispies, with a pastry blender. Then add 2 cups Rice Krispies, mixing by hand, as the mixture will be very stiff!

Make balls about the size of a marble and flatten them gently with a fork.

Bake on lightly greased cookie sheets for 10–15 minutes in a 325° oven. **(Adult)**

Can be frozen and heated up just before serving.

Cheese Popcorn

Equipment: A popcorn popper (electric) or

A large skillet with a cover

Ingredients: Popcorn kernels to pop—*one-third of a cup* should be used if you are using the skillet method.

Vegetable oil

Butter or margarine

Grated parmesan or cheddar cheese

Directions: Follow the directions with the electric popper if you are using one, or heat the skillet with one tablespoon of vegetable oil in it until it is hot, but not smoking. **An adult should handle this process.**

Add the one-third cup of corn kernels and place the lid on the skillet.

Gently slide the skillet back and forth over the burner until you can no longer hear any more kernels popping.

Empty the popped corn into a bowl, and repeat process if more popped corn is needed.

Toss the warm popcorn immediately with melted butter or margarine and either grated Parmesan or cheddar cheese. **Children supervised can help toss.**

Cinnamon Toast

Equipment: Some provision for toasting bread: an oven, a broiler oven, or a toaster; and an oven for keeping it warm. **(Used only by an adult.)**

Ingredients: A slice of bread for each child
Softened butter or margarine
A mixture of cinnamon and sugar in 1:3 ratio

Directions: Place bread on baking sheet. Place in a hot broiler (or toaster, etc.) with the tops of the bread about three inches from the source of heat. Toast until golden brown. Remove bread from broiler and turn slices over.

Spread softened butter or margarine on the toasted bread and sprinkle with the cinnamon-sugar mixture. Keep warm in oven until ready to serve. Cut in half diagonally.

Comments: Especially good on cold winter days with hot cocoa.

Country Corn Muffins or Cornbread

Equipment: Muffin pans (with optional paper liners) or:
8-inch square or round baking pan
Three medium-size mixing bowls
Rotary beater

Ingredients: 1 cup stone ground yellow cornmeal
1 cup unbleached all-purpose flour
2 teaspoons baking powder
½ teaspoon salt
2 tablespoons sugar
2 eggs separated and at room temperature
3 tablespoons vegetable oil
1 cup buttermilk

Directions: In one of the mixing bowls, stir together the cornmeal, flour, baking powder, salt, and sugar. In another bowl, beat egg yolks, then stir in oil and buttermilk. In a third bowl, beat egg white (at room temperature) with rotary beater until soft, moist peaks are formed.

Add egg yolk mixture to cornmeal mixture, stirring *only enough* to moisten the dry ingredients. Fold egg whites lightly into batter. Spoon batter into greased or paper-lined muffin pan or into greased 8-inch square or round baking pan. Fill each muffin cup about ⅔ full.

Bake in a 400° oven for 20 to 25 minutes, or until a wooden pick inserted in the center of bread comes out clean. **(Adult)**

Yields: 12 muffins or equal amount of squares or wedges

Comments: American Indians introduced the idea of cornbread to the earliest colonists. Today there are as many different kinds of cornbread as there are regions in the country.

Cornbread is good plain or served with honey or jelly.

Cornbread or muffins can also be prepared from a packaged mix.

Crunchy Cereal Mix

Equipment: Large low, flat pan

Small pan to melt butter or margarine

Covered jar or can if the mix is to be saved

Ingredients: ¼ lb. butter or margarine

2 tablespoons Worcestershire Sauce

3 drops Tabasco sauce

1 box of prepared cereal such as Rice, Wheat, or Corn Chex, Cheerios, etc. (or the equivalent of one box mixed). No pre-sweetened cereals or flaked cereals should be used.

Small thin pretzel sticks

Nuts (optional)

¼ cup grated cheese or garlic salt to taste

Directions: Melt butter or margarine over low heat. Add Worcestershire sauce and Tabasco sauce. Place cereal in a large low, flat pan. Drizzle butter mixture over and mix well. Heat in 300° oven for 45 minutes; stirring often. **(Adult supervision)**

Immediately on removing from oven, sprinkle with grated cheese *or* garlic salt. Serve hot or cold.

This cereal mix can be stored in a tightly covered can or jar.

Comments: The cereal mix can be a combination of leftovers that can be served without baking; use your own imagination.

Mini Pizzas

Equipment: One or more large baking sheets

Waxed paper

Ingredients: Refrigerated pan-ready biscuits or English muffin halves or just plain slices of white bread.

Shredded mozzarella or cheddar cheese.

Tomato sauce mixed with tomato paste, half and half.

Grated parmesan (optional)

Dried oregano (optional)

Directions: If using refrigerated pan-ready biscuits, give each child a piece of waxed paper and let him flatten the biscuit with his or her hands. Spoon on tomato sauce mixture; then sprinkle with shredded mozzarella or cheddar cheese. A pinch of dried oregano on top is an optional addition.

Put onto an ungreased pan and place in a pre-heated 400° oven for about 8–10 minutes. **(Adult)**

Variations: If you wish to use both shredded and grated cheese, put the shredded cheese onto the biscuit first; then add the tomato sauce; and finally the grated Parmesan cheese and pinch of oregano.

Bake as above.

Monkey Bread

Equipment: Bundt pan
Bowls (small)
Small pan

Ingredients: 4 cans (10 biscuits in each) refrigerated buttermilk biscuits
1½ sticks of butter or margarine
3 cups brown sugar
4 tablespoons cinnamon

Directions: Combine the brown sugar and the cinnamon, divide the mixture in half and put it into two separate bowls.

Melt one stick of butter or margarine in the small pan over low heat. **(Adult)**

Tear each biscuit into three pieces and roll into balls. Dip the balls in the melted butter and then into one bowl of the brown sugar and cinnamon mixture. Roll them around to coat evenly.

Put into the ungreased Bundt pan.

Meanwhile, melt over low heat, the second ½ stick of butter with the brown sugar/cinnamon mixture. Pour evenly and immediately over the coated balls in the Bundt pan. **(Adult)**

Bake for 30 minutes in a 350° oven.

Turn oven off. Let pan sit for 5 minutes, and then remove from oven and turn pan over on a serving plate.

Let it sit for a few minutes upside down on the plate before removing the pan.

Cool before serving.

Nachos

Equipment: Shallow baking dish or pan
Cheese grater or purchase cheese already shredded

Ingredients: Bag of corn chips
Jar of salsa
Shredded cheddar cheese

Directions: Spread corn chips in baking dish or pan. Sprinkle grated cheese over the top. Drizzle several small teaspoons of salsa (mild or medium spicy) over the top.
Bake in a 350° oven until cheese is melted. **(Adult)**
Serve right from the baking dish.

Navajo Bread

Equipment: Electric fry pan or large skillet
Bowl for mixing
Surface to flatten the dough

Ingredients: 1 cup flour
½ teaspoon salt
½ teaspoon baking powder
1 tablespoon dry milk (optional)
Water to mix with dry ingredients
Cooking oil

Directions: Mix together the flour, salt, baking powder, and dry milk. Add enough water so dough holds together but is not sticky. Break off golf-ball-sized pieces of dough and flatten into pancake shapes. Fry in oil which is heated, but not smoking. Fry until brown. **Adult should heat the oil, and do the cooking.**

Cooking time varies according to how crispy or chewy you like the bread.

Yields: 4 cakes

Open Cheese Sandwiches

Equipment: Oven to broil in **(used only by an adult)**

Foil-covered cookie sheets

Ingredients: 1 slice of bread for each child

1 slice of cheese (cheddar or American) for each child

Directions: Toast each slice of bread on one side only.

Cover untoasted side of bread with one slice of cheese.

Arrange sandwiches on foil covered cookie sheets. Place on broiler rack of oven. Set temperature control at Broil.

Sandwiches should be 2–3 inches from source of heat. Broil until cheese is slightly melted. Remove and cut into four squares or four triangles.

Serve while warm.

Peanut Butter Reindeer

Equipment: Knife for spreading peanut butter

Knife to cut bread—**used with supervision**

Ingredients: Peanut butter

Raisins

Candied cherries sliced in half

Regular pretzels—one for each reindeer

Slices of white or whole wheat bread

Directions:

1. Cut the slices of bread in half on the diagonal. Crusts may be left on or off.

2. Spread each diagonal piece of bread with peanut butter.

3. Break each pretzel in half carefully so that the resulting pieces resemble the antlers of a reindeer.

4. With the diagonal cut as the top of the reindeer's head, put the pretzel "antlers" in place; add raisin eyes, and place a candied cherry (already sliced in half) rounded side up on the bread as a nose.

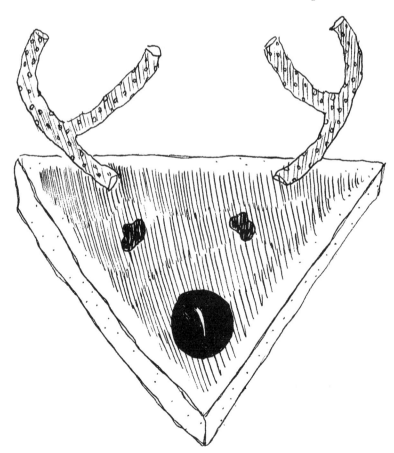

Comments: Fun and good enough so you should probably prepare two per child.

Pretzels

Equipment: Cup or small bowl
Measuring cup
Cookie sheets or flat pans

Ingredients: 1 package of active dry yeast
1½ cups warm water
1 teaspoon salt
1 tablespoon sugar
4 cups flour
1 egg beaten (or more if needed)
Coarse salt

Directions: Dissolve the yeast in warm water. Add 1 teaspoon salt and 1 tablespoon of sugar and 4 cups of flour. Knead the dough until smooth, adding more flour (up to 1 cup) if dough is sticky.

Divide dough into walnut-size pieces. Each child rolls his ball into a 12- to 14-inch rope. Shape like pretzels or any way children like. Brush them with beaten egg and sprinkle with coarse salt. Let rest on cookie sheet (uncovered) for 15 minutes. Bake at 425° for 15–18 minutes. **(Adult)**

Pumpkin Nut Bread

Equipment: Large mixing bowl
Flour sifter
9 × 5 loaf pan or two 7½ × 3¾ mini-loaf pans

Ingredients: 2 cups flour
2 teaspoons baking powder
½ teaspoon baking soda
1 teaspoon salt
1 teaspoon cinnamon
1 cup canned pumpkin
1 cup sugar
½ cup milk
2 eggs, slightly beaten
¼ cup butter or margarine, softened
1 cup chopped walnuts or pecans

Directions: Pre-heat oven to 350°. Sift together the first 5 ingredients. In a big mixing bowl, combine pumpkin, sugar, milk and eggs. Add dry ingredients and butter, mixing until just moistened. Stir in nuts. Spoon into a well-greased loaf pan. Bake 60 minutes (45 minutes for mini-loaf pans), or until wooden pick inserted in center comes out clean. Cool 10 minutes and then remove from pan. **An adult should operate the oven.**

Sandwich Cut-outs

Equipment: Different shaped cookie cutters (with good sharp edges) or a sharp knife to make squares, triangles, diamonds and other straight-sides shapes. **Supervise the use of sharp knives.**

Knives to spread fillings.

Ingredients: White bread (sliced)

Whole wheat bread (sliced)

Peanut butter, cream cheese, jelly, or other suitable sandwich fillings.

Directions: With cookie cutters or the sharp knives, cut out shapes from half of the white bread. Cut out the identical shapes from half of the whole wheat bread. Fit the whole wheat cut-outs into the holes in white slices and the white cut-outs into the cut whole wheat slices.

Spread the remaining bread (both white and whole wheat) with desired filling and place a two-toned sandwich cut-out piece on top of each.

Banana Boats

Equipment: Aluminum foil
Small knife—**used with supervision**

Ingredients: Bananas with skins left on
Miniature marshmallows
Chocolate chips

Directions: Slit open one side of the skin of the banana. Fill the crack with bits of marshmallows and chocolate chips.

Wrap each banana in aluminum foil and heat in a 400° oven for 7 minutes. The bananas can also be heated in a bed of coals for an outdoor treat.

Eat with a spoon straight out of the skin (boat). As good as a banana split!

Easy Pudding Recipes

Equipment: A collection of baby food jars with lids.

Measuring spoons

Spoons for eating the pudding

Ingredients: Instant pudding mix—chocolate, vanilla, etc.

Milk

Directions: Put 3 teaspoons (1 tablespoon) of instant pudding mix in each baby food jar. Fill jar with milk. Put lid on tightly and shake vigorously for several minutes.

Remove the lid and eat it right from the jar.

Variation: Instant pudding mix can also be prepared according to the directions on the box and then spooned into ice cream cups for serving "pudding cones."

Finger Jello

Equipment: Large bowl
Large shallow baking pan
Spatula to remove gelatin from pan

Ingredients: 4 envelopes unflavored gelatin
3 packages (3 oz. each) flavored gelatin
4 cups boiling water

Directions: In a large bowl, combine unflavored gelatin and flavored gelatin; add boiling water and stir until gelatin dissolves. Pour into large shallow pan (15½ × 10½ × 1). **Supervised by adult.**

Chill until firm. Cut into squares or triangles or use cookie cutters to get other interesting shapes. Remove carefully with a spatula.

Yield: 100 one-inch squares

Fruit Cocktail Popsicles

Equipment: Small paper cups, 5 oz. size
Popsicle sticks

Ingredients: Cans of fruit cocktail (some markets carry the very large cans)

Directions: Spoon the fruit and syrup directly from the can into the small paper cups. Fill ⅔ full.

Add a popsicle stick and freeze.

Each cup should contain some fruit and some syrup.

The popsicle stick will stand upright because you can wedge it between the pieces of fruit.

Unmold when frozen and serve.

Gingerbread

Gingerbread was an Early American favorite. Molasses from the West Indies made it especially good.

Equipment: 9-inch baking pan or muffin tins with twelve-inch 2½-inch cups
Shortening to grease the pans; or paper cup liners for muffins
Flour sifter

Ingredients: ½ cup shortening
2 tablespoons sugar
1 egg
1 cup dark molasses
1 cup boiling water **(Adult)**
2¼ cups sifted flour
1 teaspoon baking soda
½ teaspoon salt
1 teaspoon ginger
1 teaspoon cinnamon

Directions: Mix together ½ cup shortening, 2 tablespoons sugar and 1 egg. Blend in 1 cup molasses and 1 cup boiling water.

Sift together the 2¼ cups flour, 1 teaspoon soda, ½ teaspoon salt, 1 teaspoon ginger and 1 teaspoon cinnamon and add to the other ingredients, beating until smooth.

Pour into a greased 9-inch baking pan or into muffin cups (fill ⅔ full). Bake at 325° for 45 to 50 minutes.

Cut in squares.

Yield: 9–12 squares or 12 muffins.

Additional tips: Gingerbread is good with applesauce or canned pears or apricots.
Can also be prepared from a packaged mix.

Krispy Marshmallow Squares

(No Bake)

Equipment: Double boiler—2 quart size
12 × 8 × 2 inch pan
Shortening or margarine to grease pan
Large bowl

Ingredients: ¼ cup butter or margarine
2½ dozen marshmallows
5½ oz. package of Rice Krispies

Directions: Cook butter or margarine and marshmallows over hot water until soupy. Stir briskly into the cereal in a large greased bowl. **(Adult)**
Press into a greased 12 × 8 × 2 pan.
Cook, cut, and serve.

Yields: 2 dozen 2½-inch squares

No-Bake Lollipops

Equipment: Double boiler—2 quart size—**used only by an adult**
Waxed paper
Short thin plastic straws

Ingredients: one—6 oz. package semi-sweet chocolate pieces
¼ cup corn syrup
1¾ cups bite-size shredded rice or wheat cereal
Flaked coconut or ground nuts

Directions: Melt chocolate with syrup in top of a double boiler, blend well. Remove from heat, keeping chocolate mixture over hot water. Gently mix in shredded rice cereal until well coated. Drop by heaping teaspoonfuls onto waxed paper; sprinkle with coconut or ground nuts.
When cool, insert short thin plastic straws.

Oatmeal Spice Drops

Equipment: Large mixing bowl
Cookie sheets
Wire racks for cooling cookies

Ingredients: 1½ cups sifted flour
¾ teaspoon ground cinnamon
¼ teaspoon ground nutmeg
¼ teaspoon ground cloves
¼ teaspoon baking soda
¾ cup shortening
1¼ cups firmly packed brown sugar
1 egg
2 teaspoons vanilla extract
¾ cup canned pumpkin
1 ¾ cups quick or old-fashioned oats, uncooked
¾ cup salted sunflower kernels
½ cup raisins

Directions: Pre-heat oven to 375°. Sift together flour, spices, and baking soda. In large mixing bowl, cream shortening. Gradually add sugar. Cream until light and fluffy. Add egg and vanilla; mix well. Add pumpkin and flour mixture alternately; beat until thoroughly blended. Stir in oats, sunflower kernels, and raisins. Drop teaspoons of dough on ungreased cookie sheets about 1½ inches apart. Bake 15 minutes or until firm and golden brown. Remove from cookie sheets; cool on wire racks.

Yields: 4 dozen cookies

Snow Crackers

Equipment: Large baking sheet
Rotary beater or electric mixer **(Supervise electric mixer.)**
Medium sized bowl

Ingredients: 24 soda crackers
2 egg whites
¼ cup sugar
¼ teaspoon vanilla

Directions: Arrange on a baking sheet, 24 soda crackers.

Beat 2 egg whites with a rotary beater until frothy. Gradually beat in ¼ cup sugar and beat until stiff. Stir in ¼ teaspoon of vanilla. Spoon "snow" onto crackers. Spread to the edge of each cracker.

Bake at 400° for 6 to 8 minutes. Bake until golden brown (do not over-bake!). **(Adult)**

Toaster ovens work great for this recipe.

Making Butter

Equipment: A collection of baby food jars

A bowl of ice

A smaller bowl to sit in ice

Spoon to press the butter on the bowl

Measuring spoon

Ingredients: Whipping cream or heavy cream

Directions: Put 2 tablespoons of whipping cream (or no more than half of jar) in each baby food jar. Put lid on tightly and shake vigorously for as long as you can.

Remove lid and pour off excess liquid. Spoon the butter into the smaller bowl and set this bowl into the bowl of ice.

As butter chills, continue to press it against the sides of the bowl to get rid of any remaining liquid. When this is accomplished, it is ready to eat.

Hot Spiced Cider

Equipment: 5 or 6 quart kettle
Mugs or cups for serving

Ingredients: 1 gallon apple cider
four 2½–3 inch cinnamon sticks
24 whole cloves
½ teaspoon nutmeg

Directions: Combine all of the above ingredients in the large kettle.
Bring to a boil over high heat. **(Cooked and served by an adult.)**
Cover, reduce heat, and simmer for 25–30 minutes.
Strain out and discard the whole spices.
Serve in mugs or cups.

Yields: 16 servings

Easy Spreads

Crackers with peanut butter

Crackers with cheese

Graham crackers with frosting (decorated)

Graham crackers with butter (decorated)

Potato chips with cottage cheese

Bagels with cream cheese

Homemade Yogurt

Equipment: A pan to heat milk

Glass jars (baby food jars) or earthenware bowls to hold finished yogurt

Large pot or deep flat pan to hold the jars or bowls of yogurt while processing

A whisk or rotary beater and a rubber scraper

Plastic wrap

A candy or cooking thermometer

Ingredients: Quart of milk (you can use skim, low-fat, 2 percent or whole milk)

⅔ cup of powdered skim milk (dry)

1 heaping tablespoon starter (commercial yogurt)

Directions: Combine milk and powdered milk in the sauce pan. Heat milk until it is almost boiling. Watch it so that it does not boil. **(Adult)**

Remove milk from heat and cool to 115° or until milk feels comfortably warm on wrist.

While milk is cooling, remove yogurt starter from refrigerator to bring it to room temperature.

Fill the clean containers (jars or bowls) with hot water to warm them. **Supervise this process carefully.**

When milk has cooled to about 115°, add ½ cup to the yogurt starter, mixing quickly and smoothly.

Pour starter mixture into the pot of milk; quickly and gently whisk the mixture until yogurt is blended with the milk.

Pour the milk mixture into the warmed containers, filling each container to about the same level. Cover containers tightly with lids or plastic wrap. Place containers in the large pot or pan and pour hot water into the pot around the jars to within 1 inch of the yogurt level. Cover the pot and place it in the oven (no heat on) for 3 hours, or until the yogurt starts to thicken. **(Adult assistance needed.)**

Refrigerate. The yogurt will continue to thicken.

Yields: 1 quart yogurt

Additional tips: If you are using commercial yogurt for a starter, be sure to use a brand with a *live* culture. Do not use flavored yogurt as a starter.

The quicker the milk ferments into yogurt, the milder the taste. Do not let yogurt ferment longer than 5 hours or it will toughen.

Do not jiggle the yogurt while it is fermenting. The bacteria do not perform well when shaken up.

Add flavorings or fruits of choice to yogurt after it has been refrigerated.

6

SPECIAL ACTIVITIES

Every program director who has faced a sudden rainy day confining everyone inside, or who has listened to kids who are bored with day-to-day routines, knows how good it feels to be able to suggest something "special to do today."

This chapter provides directions for making unusual things like acetate slides or filmstrips, or for rigging a sheet and doing shadow sketching.

It also includes card games and useful knots for quiet times and for individual or small group activities.

Humorous stories to be acted out also become favorites to be repeated again and again.

Acetate Slides

Ages: 8–10 years and up

Materials & Equipment: Sheets of clear treated acetate for making slides (available in art supply stores; also comes in colors)

Sharpie® markers in different colors

2-inch slide frames (mounts) which can be purchased in any photo store

Electric iron **(use with adult supervision)**

Scissors

Slide projector

Directions: Cut acetate squares exactly the size to fit *inside* the green line, inside the frame. Iron closed, making sure the iron touches only the frame. Illustrate on the resulting slide using Sharpie® pens.

Variation: Two sheets of acetate squares can be used as a "sandwich" for tiny, flat objects inside, such as blades of grass or flowers, string, or paper patterns.

Comments: Patterns or designs in color make very effective slides.

Variations: The slides could also represent the moods or different parts of a short piece of music. Then slides and music could be presented together when the project is completed.

A simple tale or story might also be illustrated and then narrated as the slides are shown.

Filmstrips

Ages: 8–10 years and up

Materials & Equipment: Old filmstrips (available in many schools or film libraries)
Fine point felt-tip pens of many colors
Bleach and water
Filmstrip projector
Paper and towels
Glass mixing bowl
Soft cloths

Directions: To strip the old filmstrips, soak in a strong solution of household bleach and water (half water, half bleach), using a glass container, such as a Pyrex™ mixing bowl. **Be careful not to splatter bleach solution outside of bowl!**

Remove, rinse and wipe the filmstrip clean. If the filmstrip does not wipe clean, soak it a little longer. Use soft cloths when wiping.

Write "Start" on one frame to know the beginning from the end of the strip. Then leave a 10-inch piece of leader at the front end of the strip for threading it through the filmstrip projector.

Draw a picture for every four sprocket holes (this creates one filmstrip frame). About 22 pictures will complete a strip.

Comments: Patterns or colorful designs will probably be the easiest task to attempt in this media. Each child could do one frame or more, depending on the number of old filmstrips available.

Color Lifts

Ages: 8–10 years and up

Materials & Equipment:
Clear contact paper
Scissors and rulers
Small magazine pictures (smooth, shiny-surfaced)
Type 127 slide frames (mounts) (available at photo shops)
Electric iron **(use with adult supervision)**
Plastic wrap
Slide projector
Basin of water
Cotton balls
Hard paper towels

Directions:
Cut 2 × 2-inch squares of clear contact paper.

Place the sticky side down over the small section of the shiny magazine picture; press with ruler, rubbing gently.

Cut around the square.

Soak in water for a couple of minutes.

Rub off pulp from back of picture using cotton ball. Rub pulp off cleanly but allow picture pigment to remain.

Blot dry with a hard paper towel.

Cut 2 × 2-inch squares of plastic wrap and place one square on the back of each sticky side of the contact paper (this prevents slide from picking up lint).

Mount on #127 slide frames by ironing. Make sure the iron touches *only* the slide frame (mount).

Comments:
The children will have an array of different picture impressions transferred to their newly created slides. It might be interesting for children to decide in what order the slides might be shown to make an effective presentation. Music might be added to further enhance the project.

Shadow Sketching

Ages: 6 years and up (Children under 6 can do the activity without the sketching.)

Materials & Equipment: Large flat white cloth sheet

Twine (two pieces, about 2 feet each)

A bright light (a filmstrip projector is a good source of light)

Drawing paper or newsprint (12 × 18 inches)

Primary pencils

Clipboards (masonite pieces as big as a desk top and large paper clips). If not available, use table tops or smooth floor surface to draw on.

Directions:

1. Tie twine to two corners of the fabric sheet.
2. Suspend the sheet by tying the two corners to two high points in the room. The sheet could also be suspended from a clothesline, a wire, or a long wooden rod. The full surface of the sheet needs to be visible in order to see a person's entire shadow.
3. Set up a bright light or filmstrip projector, adjusting the height and the distance from the sheet to obtain a complete shadow (see diagram).
4. Choose one child to go behind the sheet (see diagram). Remind him/her to stay close to the sheet in order to project the best shadow.
5. Ask the child to move back and forth behind the sheet until someone says, "Freeze!" The child then holds the pose while all the other children on the other side of the sheet imitate the model's pose.
6. Ask the shadow model to move again in different ways until someone again says, "Freeze!" Everyone then tries to assume the new pose. Give each child a chance to be the model before adding the sketching activity.

(Continued)

7. Pass out the primary pencils and two or three sheets of drawing paper (attached to clipboards, if available).

8. Choose one child again to be the model, and when he/she is in a frozen position, the rest of the children sketch on their drawing paper the outline of shadow's body in this pose.

9. Sketch several different poses.

Comments: Verbalize to children a little about how the body parts look in their frozen positions—bent knees, raised arms, tilted head, etc. It will help them as they sketch.

If the group is doing well, use two models behind the sheet and sketch the interaction between the two.

Music could be added to the game activity. When the music stops the shadow freezes in its pose and everyone must imitate it.

Card Games with Regular Cards

General information:

Ages: 6–10 years for "Authors," "Old Maid," and "I Doubt It"

8 years and up for "Hearts," "Solitaire," and "Klondike" (Seven Card Solitaire)

Equipment: Decks of regular playing cards (52 cards). All of the above games can be played without special game cards.

Comments: Some of these games are simplified versions of classic card games. Changes have been made to make them easier or adaptive to regular cards. For example, "Authors" is not really the classic "Authors" game, but is played *like* "Authors." All games help develop thinking strategies, thoughtful decisions, memory, and number facts. Some of the games can be played in small groups, some by one or two children.

AUTHORS

Ages: 6–10 years

Equipment: Deck of regular playing cards

Number of Players: 4–7

Directions: Shuffle the cards and deal all of them, one at a time, around the table to each player. If some players have one more card than others, it doesn't matter.

Each player sorts his or her cards by denomination (all ones together, all sixes, all queens, etc.). The dealer then begins the game by asking any one of the other players for a card of the same denomination as he holds in his hand. He *also names the suit* that he wants. Example: Dealer holds a 10 of clubs. He asks, "Do you have a ten of hearts?" If the player has the card, she hands it over, and the dealer continues his turn and asks that player or another player for another card, again naming the denomination and suit of a denomination he holds in his hand.

If the player asked does not have the card, it becomes her turn to ask for a card she wants to match one or more she already has in her hand. As soon as a player succeeds in acquiring four cards of the same denomination, she shows them, then lays them on the table in front of her, face down. The person who has the greatest number of tricks (groups of four like cards) at the end of the game is the winner.

Hearts

Ages: 8 years and up

Equipment: Deck of regular playing cards

Number of Players: 4–6

Directions: The ranking of the cards from high to low is: A K Q J 10 9 8 7 6 5 4 3 2.

Shuffle the cards and deal an equal number of cards to each player. (Leftover cards, if any, can be removed.)

The object of the game is to avoid getting any hearts in the tricks taken.

The dealer leads a card and everyone must follow suit, if able. If a player cannot follow suit, he or she may discard anything she wishes, usually one of her high heart cards.

Examples:

1. Dealer leads a 10 of clubs. Every player adds a club card of some sort and the highest club takes the trick (look at the ranking of cards at the beginning of directions).
2. Dealer leads a 10 of clubs. All but one player add a club card. The one player without a club card plays a king of hearts. The highest club card takes the trick and is stuck with the king of hearts, which will count as points against him.

The winner of the trick leads off with the next card. The game continues with each player working to get rid of her hearts and trying to take only tricks that will not score points against her.

After all the cards have been played the players count the hearts in each of their piles.

The one with the lowest count wins.

I Doubt It

Ages: 6–10 years

Equipment: Deck of regular playing cards

Number of Players: 4–6

Directions: Shuffle the 52 cards and deal an equal number of cards to each player one at a time around the table. Put the remaining cards (if any) in the middle of the table face down.

The dealer begins the game by laying on the table in front of her, *face down*, any three cards from her own hand, saying, "These are three queens" or "These are three fours" or whatever denomination she chooses. Each player in turn, starting on the left, has the chance to challenge her and say "I doubt it," meaning he doesn't believe they are the three cards the dealer has named, or he can pass without saying anything.

If a player says "I doubt it," the three cards are turned face up. If the three cards are not what the dealer said they were, she must not only take those three cards back into her hand, but must take all the cards on the table at the time (including the center pile).

If the three cards *are* what the dealer said they were, the one who said "I doubt it" must take the three cards and all the cards remaining on the table.

The next player to the left of the dealer then lays down three cards and claims that they are three of a certain denomination; and so the game continues.

When a player doesn't have three cards left, he must take one from the table to make three. If there are none on the table, he must pass and wait until his turn comes again.

If no one doubts a namer's statement, the three cards are not shown and are left face down on the table. The play then moves to the next person on the left of most recent namer.

The first player to get rid of all his or her cards is the winner.

Solitaire

Ages: 8 years and up

Equipment: Deck of regular playing cards

Number of Players: 1

Directions: The object of this game is to get the cards out of the hand in sequence and suit and build upon common foundations. Ranking is from low to high: A 2 3 4 5 6 7 8 9 10 J Q K.

First, pick out the four aces and lay them in a row for the foundations. You will now build upon these, in sequence and matching suit, up to the King.

Example:

The next card to add to this pile will be the 2 of hearts, then the 3, etc. up to the king.

Shuffle the rest of the cards and deal them one at a time, face up, using any card that is appropriate for building on a foundation. Cards not usable are placed face up in piles below the four aces. No more than four piles may be formed, but the non-usable cards may be placed in any of the four piles and the top card of any pile may be taken at any time for placement on a foundation.

When all of the pack cards have been dealt, and all of the four piles have been used the game is at an end.

The object of course is to complete each foundation up to the king, if possible, or to see how far one can get.

Variation:

Two players may play "Double Solitaire." They sit across the table from one another and play on their own or each other's foundations. Two decks of cards are needed for this version.

Instead of four aces to play on, there are eight in the center. Players may use only their own cards to shuffle and play on all the aces.

Old Maid

Ages: 6–10 years

Equipment: Deck of regular playing cards

Number of Players: 4–6

Directions: Remove the Queen of Hearts from a 52-card pack and shuffle the remaining cards.

Deal the cards one at a time around the table to each player until the whole pack is dealt out. The players then sort their cards into pairs, and all pairs are put down on the table in front of them, face up. Four cards of a kind become two pairs.

The first player offers his or her remaining cards face down, and spread out like a fan, to the player on his left, who draws one.

If it makes a pair, the pair is placed face up in front of the second player. That player (whether she has gotten a pair or not) then offers the cards remaining in her hand face down, to the player on her left. This is continued until only one card is left (which has to be the odd queen).

Comments: If you feel the title of this game is sexist, you could change its name. Also, the person who holds the odd queen at the end could be called "The Cheese" instead of the "Old Maid."

Klondike or Seven-Card Solitaire

Ages: 8 years and up

Equipment: Deck of regular playing cards

Number of Players: 1

Directions: Shuffle the pack of 52 cards and turn up the top card and lay it down on the table in front of you face up. Then lay six more cards in a row to the right of this card but keep these cards facing down. (See illustration)

On the second card of the top row, place another card face up this time and then continue placing five cards face down on the rest of the cards.

On the third card of the top row place one card face up and then continue placing four cards face down on the rest of the piles.

Continue as above, each time moving one more card to the right until you have reached the seventh pile and placed a card, facing up, thereon. The remaining cards are called the "pack."

The piles can be stacked but this is what each should contain:

The starters are always aces and the moment they appear, whether in the cards in front or in the pack, they are put in a line by themselves at the top of the layout.

On these aces, sequence and suit of cards are built up to kings. (Same suit, same color; Ace is low, king is high.)

Before you begin working with the rest of the pack of cards, the player should begin working with the piles in front of him or her. These piles are all built downward and always alternate color, red and black.

Example: Pile 2 might have a black ten on it and pile 7 might have a red jack on it. Move the black ten to the red jack and turn up the face-down card left in pile 2. If it is an ace, move it to the space above the layout and start to build on it, if possible. Remember, on the aces you must go in sequence upward to the king and stay in the same suit (hearts, diamonds, clubs and spades). In the empty space left in pile 2 you can fill it only with a king.

You may not move a card from a pile unless it is face up on the pile. You may, however, move *all* the face-up cards on one pile onto another pile.

Example: You could move all the face-up cards (from a black nine down to a red four) on one pile to a red ten on another pile.

When you have exhausted all the possible moves with your beginning piles, begin "running off" the remainder of the pack of cards in threes. (To "run off": hold the pack in the left hand face down. Count off the top three cards and place them face up on the table with the third card on top of the other two. You must play the top card first, if possible, to uncover the next, and the next.) Use the turned up cards as often as possible to build up or down on all piles.

Each time you run through the pack in threes and remove one or more cards, you change the cards that will turn up. When you reach an impasse and no new cards turn up, the game is at an end.

The object, of course, is to build up all of your aces to kings in sequence. Don't be discouraged if this doesn't happen too often!

Camping Trip

Rita Shotwell

Ages: 4–9 years

Benefits: Using voice inflections to emphasize words
Auditory skills

Directions: Say the poem one line at a time and have the children echo, using actions. Later, children might take turns leading the chant, or the whole class could say it together.

Story:

> We're going on a camping trip [march while saying]
> Far, far away [shade eyes with hand and look ahead]
> Got my sleeping bag [rest head on hands held at side of neck]
> Got my knapsack [hands on shoulders as if touching the straps]
> One big tent [say in deep voice]
> One tiny pillow [say in high voice]
> One lon–g walking stick [say slowly]
> One short flashlight [say fast]
> Plenty of food [rub stomach]
> But no–o–o–o soap! [move head in a circle while saying, "no"]
> O–O–O–O! [cover mouth with one hand and look surprised]

Variation:

> Clap the rhythm of the words while saying each line
> Omit the words, just clap the story.
> Clap certain lines and have children guess which line you are clapping.

Comments: For young children, the teacher could prepare picture cards with stick figures, illustrating the various lines of the chant.

The Dinosaur

Rita Shotwell

Ages: 3–6 years

Benefits: Concentration skills

Coming in on cue

Coordination of actions and words

Directions: Practice saying the words, "oh my!" while putting both hands up to sides of mouth (cheeks). Tell the children to watch you closely and every time you put your hands up to your face, they are to do the same and say, "oh my!" (with expression).

Tell the story, one line at a time and have children come in on signal.

Story:

A dinosaur walked into town

Oh my!

He walked without making a sound

Oh my!

He looked to the left, he looked to the right

Oh my!

He looked all around, it was such a sight

Oh my!

He spotted a boy, he spotted a girl

Oh my!

He started to dance, he started to twirl

Oh my!

He laughed as he ran all over the town

Oh my!

He started to jump and then he fell down

Oh my!

Variation: Have half of the group be dinosaurs and act out words. The other half of the group will say, "oh my!" as the teacher tells the story. Repeat the story and change roles so everyone has a chance to be a dinosaur.

The Elephant, Mouse, and Cat

Rita Shotwell

Ages: 4–6 years

Benefits: Auditory skills

Concentration skills

Coming in on cue

Materials & Equipment: Pictures of an elephant, a mouse, and a cat (not necessary for older children)

Hand drum (optional)

Directions: Go over the sounds for each of the animals, then tell the story and have the children make the appropriate sound when the animal is named.

Elephant: Beat hand drum or say "boom, boom, boom" with a deep voice.

Mouse: Hit side of drum with mallet or make a sound of "chewing cheese" with mouth (exaggerate sound).

Cat: Say, "meow."

Story:

Once upon a time there was a great big elephant ——— a little tiny mouse ——— and a very friendly cat.

Now the elephant ——— believe it or not, was afraid of the little tiny mouse ——— so he asked the very friendly cat ——— for help.

"Please kittycat, ask the mouse to be my friend" said the elephant ——— [speak in a deep voice]

"Well," said the very friendly cat ——— , "I'll see what I can do."

Meanwhile, the little tiny mouse ——— was out looking for the very friendly cat ——— . When he found him, he cried, "Please kittycat, ask the elephant to be my friend." [speak in a high voice]

So the very friendly cat ——— had a party and invited the elephant ——— and the mouse ——— and they all became good friends: the elephant ——— the mouse ——— and the very friendly cat ——— .

Variation: Can be acted out with three children playing the parts; or three groups of children with each group as one animal.

Jason and His Music

Rita Shotwell

Ages: 3–5 years

Benefits: Visual perception
Visual discrimination
Concentration skills

Materials: Picture of a happy and a sad face.

Directions: Show pictures to children; have them imitate a happy or sad face, depending on the picture. Tell them you are going to read them a story and they will "laugh" or "cry" when you hold up one of the pictures.

Story:

Once upon a time there was a little boy named Jason. Now Jason loved music because it made him feel very happy. [happy face]

One day, while he was listening to music, he started dancing and laughing. [happy face]

He danced and danced—and all of a sudden, he fell down. [sad face]

He hurt his little knee and he started crying. [sad face]

He cried and cried and cried. [sad face]

His Mommy came running over to kiss his knee and make him feel better. She started to tickle him to make him laugh. [happy face]

He laughed and laughed and laughed. [happy face]

He laughed so hard, he started to cry. [sad face]

Now what do you think of that? First he was laughing [happy face] and then he was crying! [sad face]

All of a sudden his Daddy turned the radio on and Jason heard the music and he started laughing. [happy face]

He danced and laughed [happy face] because he felt good all over and he was happy the rest of the day! [happy face]

Comments: Provides a good opportunity to discuss happy and sad feelings. Have the children stop "laughing" or "crying" as soon as you put the picture down. This story could also be acted out by the children.

The Toy

Rita Shotwell

Ages: 5–8 years

Benefits: Auditory skills

Coming in on cue

Directions: Divide the class into four groups:

Group #1: Tell them every time you say the words, "she said," they are to say, "ooh–h–h."

Group #2: Tell them every time you say the words, "he said," they are to say, "ah–h–h."

Group #3: Tell them every time you say the words, "they said," they are to say, "eh" and shrug their shoulders.

Group #4: Quietly tell them when you get to the end of the story and say, "but the toy said . . ." they are to jump up and shout, "WOW!"

Story:

Mom found an old toy in the basement. When she showed it to the children,

She said, "ooh–h–h"
He said, "ah–h–h"
They said, "eh!"

Mom wound the toy up and when it started to move,

She said, "ooh–h–h"
He said, "ah–h–h"
They said, "eh!"

The toy moved around the room, the children's eyes got very big and,

She said, "ooh–h–h"
He said, "ah–h–h"
They said, "eh!"

When the toy started to spin,

She said, "ooh–h–h"
He said, "ah–h–h"
They said, "eh!"

The toy was spinning so fast that it fell to the ground and

She said, "ooh–h–h"
He said, "ah–h–h"
They said, "eh!"

But the toy said,

"WOW!"

Comments: Tell the story with a lot of emotion and the children's responses will be more dramatic. This can also be acted out with a fifth group being the "toys."

Oh Boy!

Rita Shotwell

Ages: 3–5 years

Benefits: Auditory skills
Use of emotions
Encourages creativity

Directions: The teacher tells the children:

> Say the words, "Oh Boy" as though you were really happy!
> Now say them as though you were really sad.
> How about mad!
> And scared!
> How about if you were a tiny little mouse?
> [say with a high voice]
> Or a great big giant [say with a deep voice]
> Now say them happy again.

After going over all of the emotions and saying "Oh Boy," read the story and have the class answer each statement with the words, "Oh Boy," with emotions that correspond with the statement.

Story:

> You are each going to receive one million dollars! [happy]
> But, in order to receive it, you must peel 10 lbs of onions! [sad]
> And eat 5 lbs of spinach! [mad, because you hate spinach!]
> And have a fight with a tiger! [scared]
> And show me a real mean face. [mad]
> And turn into a tiny mouse. [high voice]
> And a great big giant! [low voice]
> And now, you can have your money! [happy]

Extend: Older children can make up their own story and use "Oh Boy" or another signal word.

With younger children, the teacher can help children make up their story; or use other signal words in place of "Oh Boy."

Story of Colors

Rita Shotwell

Ages: 3–6 years

Benefits: Auditory skills
Following simple directions
Concentration skills
Group cooperation

Materials: Blue, red, green, and yellow construction paper, divided evenly among students.

Directions: Give each student a piece of colored construction paper. Keep each color group together.

Ask all the students with the blue paper to raise their hands, do this with each color to make sure they know what color they have.

Tell them you are going to tell a story and that they have to listen closely so as to follow the directions for each color.

Story:

As I was walking down the street, the color *BLUE* I saw. *Stand up BLUE* and *take a bow,* then *wave to us* one and all. *Sit down BLUE,* you had your turn,

now look at the color *RED. Stand up RED* and *pat your head, turn around* and *sit down.*

Along the way I saw some *GREEN,* as pretty as *GREEN* could be. *Stand up GREEN* and *jump for me. Jump* and *jump* and *touch the ground,* now you may *sit down.*

Look, I see the color *YELLOW! Stand up YELLOW* and *stretch up high. Up on your toes,* try to *reach the sky. Sit down YELLOW,* this is almost the end.

All stand up and *wiggle with your friends. Shake* and *shake* and *shake* real fast. Now it's time to rest at last!

Sit down BLUE, then *YELLOW,* then *GREEN* and *RED: Bow your heads* and *go to bed.*

Comments: Tell the story four times. Keep changing the colors for the children so they will have a new color and new directions to listen for each time.

For older children, make the directions harder and/or add more colors.

My Name Is Joe

Ages: 6 years and up

Benefits: Coordination and concentration skills

Directions: Say the chant six times, each time adding on a new body movement. By the sixth time, you will have both arms, both legs, head, whole body moving! The seventh time is the end.

Chant:

Hi, my name is Joe. I work in a button factory. One day, my boss said, "Joe, are you busy?" I said, "no." He said, "turn the button with your *right hand.*" [Start moving right hand and arm to the right in a circular motion and continue moving as you continue the chant. Children only do the actions, they don't echo the words to the chant.]

Hi, my name is Joe. I work in a button factory. One day, my boss said, "Joe, are you busy?" I said, "no." He said, "turn the button with your *left hand.*" [Start moving left hand and arm to the left in a circular motion—right hand and arm will also be moving.]

Repeat chant and add, "turn the button with your *right leg.*" [Start moving right leg to the right, making small circles with your knee—by now, both hands and right leg are moving.]

Repeat chant and add, "turn the button with your *left leg.*" [Start moving left leg to the left, making small circles with your knee. Now you have both hands and both legs moving!]

Repeat chant and add, "turn the button with your *head.*" [Start moving head up and down or in a circle (it's harder to move your head in a circle.] Now you have both hands, both legs and head moving!

Repeat chant and add, "turn the button with your *body.*" [Start moving whole body while walking in a small circle.] Now you have both hands, both legs, head and whole body moving!

Repeat chant, only this time there is a new ending:

Hi, my name is Joe, I work in a button factory. One day, my boss said, "Joe, are you busy?" I said, "Yes!" He said, "YOU'RE FIRED!!"

Comments: Some first, second and third grade students demonstrated this for us, and it certainly put everyone in a giggly mood!

Heidi High and Larry Low

Rita Shotwell

Ages: 4 years and up

Benefits: Fine motor skills
Small muscle development
Group cooperation
Group participation

Directions: Have everyone sit in chairs or kneel on the floor and sit back on their heels. Tell everyone to watch you closely and when you stand up, they stand up and when you sit down, they sit down. Also, tell them to watch your hands closely and to imitate your actions with their thumbs and also to imitate the tone of your voice. Tell the story:

"This is a story about a little girl named 'Heidi High' [say in a high voice and hold out right thumb, have children echo name in a high voice] and a little boy named, 'Larry Low' [say in a low voice and hold out left thumb, have children echo name in a low voice].

"Now each child lived in a house so we need to open the door [make a clicking sound with your tongue and spread your hands out to the sides], put them inside [make a clicking sound again and tuck thumb inside of palm], and close the door [make clicking sound again and fold fingers over thumbs].

"One day, Heidi High [say in high voice] decided to go see Larry Low [say in a low voice], so she opened the door [make clicking sound with tongue and open right hand, keeping thumb tucked inside palm], went outside [make clicking sound again and stick thumb out], and closed the door [make clicking sound again and close hand to make a fist, keeping thumb outside of fist].

"She went up a hill [say in a high voice] and down a hill [say in a low voice] and up a hill and down a hill and up a hill and down a hill [keep using high and low voice while saying] until she came to Larry's house.

[When going up and down the hill, make your voice go up and down with your thumb, move thumb right to left over to Larry's house and then, move thumb left to right to go back home. Go up and down with your body also. If you are sitting in a chair, stand up and then sit down—if you are kneeling on the floor, go up on your knees and sit back on your heels again.]

"When she got there, she knocked on the door [tap left fist with right thumb three times and make three clicking sounds]. 'Anybody home?' [say in high voice]. No one answered, so she knocked again [tap left fist again three times and make clicking sounds]. 'Anybody home?' [say again in high voice]. Still no answer, so she turned around and went up the hill and down the hill [say with high and low voice] until she got home.

"When she got home, she opened the door [make clicking sound and open right hand], went inside [tuck thumb into palm and make clicking sound] and closed the door [fold fingers over thumb while making a clicking sound].

"Right after that, Larry Low [say in low voice] came home from the store and he decided to go see Heidi High [say in a high voice] so he opened the door [make clicking sound with tongue and open left hand, keep thumb tucked inside palm] went outside [make clicking sound again and stick thumb out], closed the door [make clicking sound again and close hand to make a fist, keep thumb outside].

"He went up a hill and down a hill and up a hill and down a hill and up a hill and down a hill [say with voice going high and low and left thumb moving up and down going from left to right] until he got to Heidi's house.

"When he got there, he knocked on the door [tap right fist with left thumb three times and make three clicking sounds]. 'Anybody home?' [say in low voice]. No one answered, so he knocked again [tap left fist three times again]. 'Anybody home?' [say in low voice]. Still no answer, so he turned around and went up a hill and down a hill and up a hill and down a hill and up a hill and down a hill [say with voice going high and low and left thumb moving up and down going from right to left] until he got home.

"When he got home, he opened the door [make clicking sound and open left hand], went inside [tuck thumb into palm and make a clicking sound] and closed the door [fold fingers over thumb while making a clicking sound].

"The next day, they both woke up at the same time and both decided to go see each other, so they opened their doors [make two clicking sounds and open both hands to the side] went outside [make clicking sound again and stick thumbs out] closed their doors [make two clicking sounds again and close hands to make fists, keeping thumbs outside].

"They both went up a hill and down a hill and up a hill and down a hill and up a hill and down a hill AND THEY MET [have thumbs face each other and bend thumbs up and down] and they talked and talked and talked.

"When they were all finished, they said, "Goodbye" [high voice], "Goodbye" [low voice] and they turned around and went up a hill and down a hill and up a hill and down a hill and up a hill and down a hill until they got home.

"When they got home, they opened their doors [make two clicking sounds and open hands], went inside [make clicking sound and tuck thumbs inside palms] and closed their doors [make clicking sounds and cover thumbs with fingers] and that's the end of the story!

Extend: Change to Mrs. Witch and Mr. Ghost for Halloween. When the two meet, they carry on a conversation about Halloween (using high and low voices and bending thumbs up and down while talking).

Change to Santa Claus and Miss Pine Cone for Christmas. Their conversation involves Santa asking Miss Pine Cone to marry him (this was a suggestion from one of the Kindergarten students at Community School).

Comments: This is my version of an activity taught by Lillian Yaross at one of her workshops. Lillian is a national Orff clinician and she has always been an inspiration to me. [RS]

The Rain Storm

Ages: 3–9 years

Benefits: Use of body percussion
Motor skills
Connecting actions with words (dramatics)

Directions: Everyone stand in a circle or scatters around the room. Tell the children to raise their arms in the air. "We are going to pretend we are trees and our arms are the branches of the trees."
The teacher tells the following story:

"It's a very pretty day and the sun is shining. The trees are blowing gently in the wind [sway arms slowly from side to side].

"All of a sudden it gets very dark. The wind picks up and the trees start swaying [make the sound of the wind while swaying arms from side to side. Sway faster and make the wind sounds louder.]

"It starts to rain in little tiny drops [snap fingers for sound of rain].

"The drops get bigger [pat thighs with hands for sounds of heavier rain].

"It starts to rain very hard [pat thighs hard and fast.]

Shout: "And it starts to thunder [stamp feet real hard.]

"And lightning [clap hands very loud].

"And thunder [stamp feet again].

"And lightning [clap hands again].

"And the rain comes down very hard and fast [pat thighs hard and fast].

[Start to lower your voice]: "Then the rain slows down [pat thighs slowly]. Soon the big drops turn into little tiny drops [snap fingers]. The sun comes out [raise arms and sway, slowly, side to side] and the trees are blowing gently again."

Variation:

After acting out the rain storm, you can sing, "It's Raining, It's Pouring" and "Rain, Rain Go Away."

Comments: This has been a favorite activity of every group in which it's been tried.

Swinging Farm

Ages: 3–5 years

Benefits: Visual perception
Visual discrimination
Use of vocal sounds

Materials: Pictures of animals, insects, farm equipment.

Directions: Go over each picture and have children name the picture and make the sound that corresponds to the picture.
Next all sing the song and the teacher shows one picture. Children make the sound and act out what is in the picture. Keep singing the song until you have shown all of the pictures.

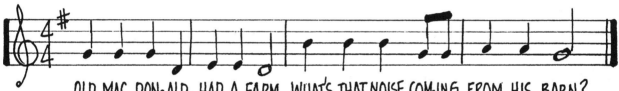

OLD MAC DON-ALD HAD A FARM. WHAT'S THAT NOISE COM-ING FROM HIS BARN?

MEOW

Comments: Put in some pictures that do not belong on a farm and see if the children can tell you where they belong—Example: elephant—zoo.
Instead of pictures, children could act out different animals.

Useful Knots

Ages: 8 and up

Comments: Everyone sometime in his life will have to tie a package tightly, attach a rope to a tree or post, join two ropes, or make a knot that won't slip. It is important to know the way to tie the knot that you need for each of the above instances.

Materials: Pieces of clothesline rope about 3 feet in length (not plastic clothesline). Ball of twine (for whipping rope ends).

General Directions: Parts of a rope:

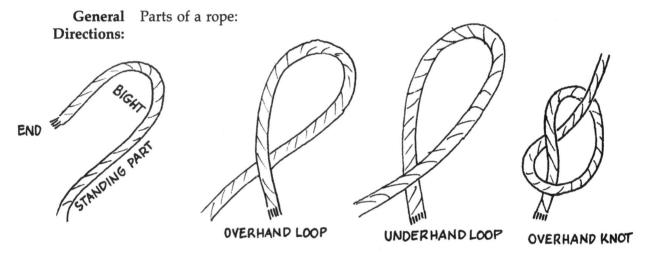

OVERHAND LOOP   UNDERHAND LOOP   OVERHAND KNOT

Whipping ends of rope (to prevent unraveling):

Cut a piece of twine 2 feet long. Make it into a big loop with ends overlapping somewhat and place this loop at the end of the rope (see diagram). Wrap the twine tightly around the rope, starting ¼ inch from the end of the rope end. When the whipping is as wide as the rope is thick, pull out the ends hard and trim off the twine. Whip the other end of the rope also.

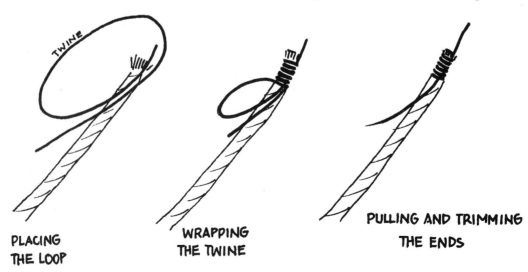

PLACING THE LOOP   WRAPPING THE TWINE   PULLING AND TRIMMING THE ENDS

Square Knot

(Used for Tying Up Packages or in First Aid Bandages)

Directions: Grab one end of your 3-foot length of rope in each hand. Cross the right hand rope end over the left hand rope and loop it under and up (see illustration). You will then notice that your rope ends have changed sides. Next, you continue by crossing the left hand rope end over the right hand rope, loop it under and pull on both ends. You have a square knot.

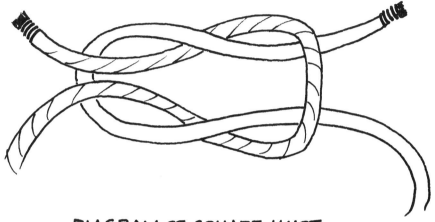

DIAGRAM OF SQUARE KNOT

Sheet Bend

A sheet bend knot is used to join two ropes together (same or different thicknesses). Example: joining several short jump ropes together to make a long one.

Directions: Bend the end of one of the ropes so that it lies beside its own standing part. You now have made a "bight" (See illustration)

Bring the end of the second rope through the bight and then around it.

Next, slip the end of this second rope under its own standing part where it enters the bight. Pull taut.

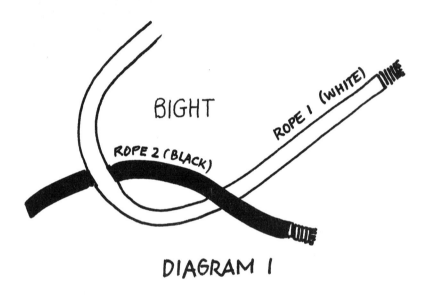

BIGHT

ROPE 1 (WHITE)

ROPE 2 (BLACK)

DIAGRAM 1

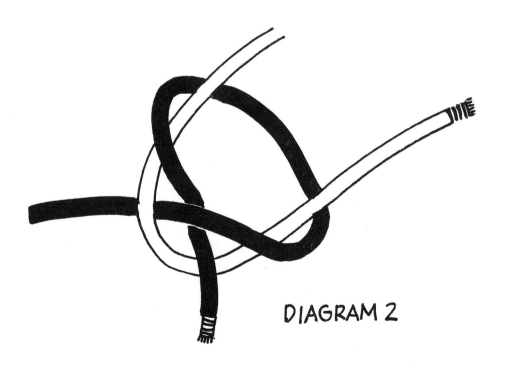

DIAGRAM 2

Bowline Knot

(Pronounced Bō-lin)

The bowline is a knot that will not slip. It is used in rescuing people in mountain, fire, and water accidents. It can also make you a loop around a pole or a tree if you're missing a jump rope "turner."

Directions: Grab your piece of rope about a half the distance from one free end to make an overhand loop (see parts of a rope).

Insert the same free end into the loop from underneath (coming out of the hole, so to speak). (Diagram 1)

Then bring the free end around the standing part (or around the "tree" to help you remember) and back down through the hole or loop. Pull taut. (Diagram 2)

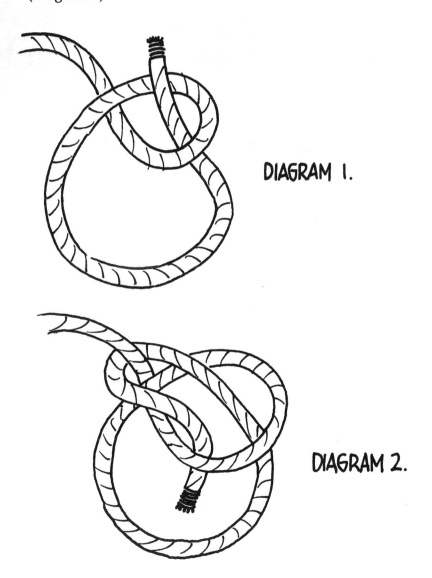

DIAGRAM 1.

DIAGRAM 2.

Index